GW00470318

Rosa richardii

The Mitchell Beazley
Pocket Guide to

Old-fashioned
Roses

Orietta Sala

MITCHELL BEAZLEY

The Mitchell Beazley Pocket Guide to Old-fashioned Roses
This edition published in 1995 by Mitchell Beazley, an imprint of Reed
Consumer Books Limited, Michelin House, 81 Fulham Road,
London SW3 6RB, and Auckland, Melbourne, Singapore and Toronto

First published in 1993
under the title Le Rosa d'Epoca
by Garzanti Editore S.p.a.

ISBN 1 85732 577 X

A CIP catalogue record for this book is available from the British Library

Designed and produced by The Bridgewater Book Company Limited
Printed and bound in France by Imprimerie Pollina SA

Contents

Rosa moschata

Introduction

Roses may be considered antique or modern in much the same fashion as furniture, furnishings and jewellery. They may have a date of birth, be of known parentage, and frequently bear the name of their creator. Most roses in cultivation have not arisen spontaneously, but may be regarded, especially by the unromantic, as manufactured products or highly sophisticated creations. They are the result of deliberate cross-pollinations, and have been produced by the lengthy process and patient work of hybridisation, with their parent plants selected for their potential contributions of colour, scent, texture and form, and for hardiness and disease resistance. A modern rose like 'Peace', enormously successful since the 1950s, is the outcome of some forty-odd crosses, which means that at least eighty roses have contributed to its conception.

There are approximately 150 known species of rose in existence, distributed throughout the temperate and subtropical regions of the northern hemisphere, from a vast area comprising Eastern and Central Asia, Europe, Africa and North America, with the greatest diversity occurring in western China. Only relatively small numbers of these have made contributions to modern garden roses, but have done so in innumerable combinations over many centuries. The Gallicas, *Rosa gallica*, the Damasks, *R. × damascena*, and Albas, *R. × alba*, in particular, along with several Chinese species, have played a very important role. Several others have contributed to the enterprise, albeit to a lesser extent, providing us with small, interesting groups of shrub roses: for example, the Sweet Briars, derived from *R. rubiginosa* and *R. foetida*, the Rugosas, from *R. rugosa*, and the Hybrid Musks, which have *R. moschata* in their distant ancestry. The rambling roses have been created with *R. multiflora*, *R. wichuraiana*, and *R. semper-virens* amongst their parent species, and climbers from *R. gigantea* and *R. moschata*. The first old varieties probably occurred spontaneously and there followed, with the passage of time, many others created by the ingenuity and application of horticulturists, gardeners and amateur rosarians. Especially from the end of the 18th century onwards varieties have been combined continuously in pursuit of ever more stunning progeny. In this way, modern roses have acquired very large blooms replete with petals, in almost every imaginable shade of colour, and with ever-longer flowering seasons.

But what exactly distinguishes an Old Garden Rose from a Modern Rose? One convention has it that the former are those created before World War One. All the others born this century from 1915 onwards are Modern Roses.

But the distinction is much more subtle and, insofar as garden use is concerned, does not concern the date of birth: the difference is their qualities and characteristics.

Modern Roses are represented principally by two well-defined, thriving categories, Hybrid Teas and Floribundas: the former are remontant or repeat-flowering shrubs with stiff stems bearing single, large blooms in the typical Tea rose shape, high-pointed in the middle with the numerous petals folding outwards, now more correctly known as large-flowered bush roses. The latter are those now called cluster-flowered bushes, with each more or less upright stem bearing

Rosa pimpinellifolia

sprays of up to 25 blooms throughout summer. Most have a formal elegance that is better suited to bedding; they are, in the words of one authority on roses, "flower-producing machines". To these two categories we must add Miniature roses and Patio roses (Dwarf cluster-flowered bush) which are becoming more and more popular given that they lend themselves to planting in pots and boxes for terraces and balconies, and Ground cover roses, trailing and spreading hybrids that root where they touch the ground. The Modern Shrub roses, amongst them Hybrid Musks, Rugosa Hybrids and David Austin's English Roses, include many which bridge the gap between the prim elegance of the Hybrid Teas and Floribundas and the more natural grace of the Old Roses, and it is for that reason that we include them here. There is an increasing appreciation of shrub roses.

We all grow or have grown these Modern Roses, above all because they are the ones that are most often recommended to us. We have always thought that they are the epitome of beauty. But if, during an outing in the country, we ever happen upon a hedgerow studded with the fragrant blooms of wild roses, we suddenly feel cheated. What happened to the roses we know, those most commonly found in gardens, to make them so different from those growing in the wild? And we begin to look at our modern creations with a feeling of disappointment, we judge them to be inadequate. The roses of the past must have had far greater powers of seduction if they have aroused so much emotion and inspired so much poetry over the centuries. The cool perfection of our Modern Roses, in contrast, seems lacking in enchantment, although their flowers are usually larger.

Old Garden Roses can bridge the enormous gulf between the delicacy of wild roses, too transient for the demands of a garden, and Modern Roses lacking in romance: they were created before "industry" managed to standardise everything it touched. They offer grace of form, a purity of tone and delicacy of colour, and abundant diversity of scent unrivalled by the sophisticated creations of the Modern Rose. Those who learn to appreciate Old Garden Roses do not ever give them up; they fall in love with them and therefore forgive their defects. Defects which really boil down to one thing only: most bear their opulent and sensually fragrant blooms in one glorious, short-lived flush in summer. Old Garden Roses, which are returning to our gardens with more and more authority, need little recommendation. Once one is persuaded to grow a few of them, they will speak eloquently for themselves. The only thing we need do is be receptive and learn to appreciate their beauty. Also, many of these roses are unusually scented and introduce a further quality to gardens, whatever their size.

OLD ROSES AND THEIR HYBRIDS

'Bourbon Queen'

O how much more doth beauty beauteous seem
By that sweet ornament which truth doth give!
The rose looks fair, but fairer we it deem
For that sweet odour which doth in it live.
The canker blooms have full as deep a dye
As the perfumèd tincture of the roses,
Hang on such thorns, and play as wantonly
When summer's breath their maskèd buds discloses;
But for their virtue only is their show
They live unwooed and unrespected fade,
Die to themselves. Sweet roses do not so;
Of their sweet deaths are sweetest odours made:
And so of you, beauteous and lovely youth,
When that shall fade, by verse distils your truth.

Wm. Shakespeare (SONNETS, 54)

Key

🌺 Continuous-flowering or repeat-flowering (remontant)

🌼 A summer flush of blooms, followed by a second, lesser flush in autumn

⊘ Spring-flowering only

◎ Summer-flowering only

🍵 Suitable for growing in pots or tubs

🥀 Display of hips in autumn

▣ Tolerant of shade

▣ Suitable for growing under glass

☼ Must have very warm, sheltered conditions

▣ Suitable for hedges

🍀 Good for ground cover

🌼 Good for bedding

✦ Suitable for north-facing walls

Note

The size of a rose bush, the flowering season, and sometimes flower colour, depend to a large extent on soil type and fertility, available moisture, and climate. The information given should be treated as a general guideline. The blooming season given is for a cool temperate climate, such as that in Great Britain. In warmer regions, flowering may occur up to one month earlier. Some roses may, therefore, begin to bloom in mid-spring in warm temperate climates.

GALLICA ROSES

Rosa gallica 'Officinalis'

A little history

If the rose is the symbol of love, then the Gallica Rose, the red rose *par excellence*, is its epitome. It brings to mind the evocative myth of Venus, who pricked her foot on a thorn in her haste to join Adonis; the drops of blood turned into red roses while from her tears white roses were born.

The Gallica Rose, *Rosa gallica*, a short, suckering bush native from southern Europe to western Asia, is almost certainly one of the first roses to be cultivated in the gardens of antiquity, not only in private gardens but also undoubtedly for commercial purposes: roses were much prized as cut flowers, but also valued for the extracted oils, attar of rose, used medicinally and in perfumery.

It is also important for the fundamental role played in the evolution of the rose: the Gallica gave rise – probably by spontaneous cross-fertilisation – to the Damasks and Albas; its chromosomes are also present in the complicated genetic make-up of the Centifolia. These roses constituted the basis on which horticulturists worked, above all in the 19th century, so as to achieve the creation of many new hybrids and, finally, the creation of today's roses. A lesser contribution, but not to be overlooked, was provided by the cross between *R. gallica* and *R. phoenicia* to yield the fragile but luminous *R. × richardii*, the Holy Rose of Abyssinia, kept in many of the Pharaohs' tombs as a sweet travelling companion for the soul on the journey to the hereafter.

The Gallica's intense perfume which persists even on drying and, perhaps primarily, its medicinal virtues – astringent and anti-inflammatory – have contributed to its endurance,

Rosa gallica 'Versicolor'

especially during the dark centuries of the Middle Ages, when ornamental flowers were afforded little consideration, other than in convent cloisters and monastic herb gardens. It re-emerges in literature post-1000 AD, in the writings of Albertus Magnus and Petrus Crescentius. In Europe, we see it triumphant in the form of *Rosa gallica* 'Officinalis', the Apothecary's Rose, probably brought back from Damascus to France by the crusaders in the 13th century; Thibaut Le Chansonnier, the Count of Champagne, is credited with bringing it to Provins, which became the principal centre for its cultivation, hence its alternative name, Rose of Provins. 'Officinalis' is not alone in acquiring fame; so did the double-flowered mutation, Rosa Mundi, *R. gallica* 'Versicolor', with petals striped and flaked with white, pink and red, that probably originated in Norfolk, England, during the 16th century.

By the close of the 16th century there are numerous references to the Gallica Rose in botanical texts of the period, from William Turner to Lobelius, John Gerard's *Herbal* and John Parkinson's *Paradisi in Sole Paradisus Terrestris*, which describes twelve varieties in 1629.

The Gallica is probably the rose most fêted by literature and poetry, religion and heraldry, an emblem with diverse symbolic significance: it was the sacred rose of the Medes and Persians, the incarnation of both profane and sacred Love, and was the royal rose of England and the red rose of Lancaster. Garlands of red roses frequently frame the Madonna in the paintings of the 15th and 16th centuries.

It is a reasonable supposition, therefore, that for all of this period, the rose was also grown in gardens. It was during the reign of Empress Josephine, however, at the beginning of the 19th century, that the Gallicas probably reached their peak; in Josephine's garden near Paris two hundred different forms of Gallica could be admired.

Of all the hundreds of varieties that were created in the 19th century, many have fallen into oblivion; but those described here have resisted the assault of time.

Characteristics

Rosa gallica is a vigorous, dense, upright shrub, seldom more than 1.2m (4ft) in height, with green or red-tinted stems clothed in slender, sometimes hooked, prickles and bristles. The leaves, with 3–7 broadly elliptic or rounded leaflets, are smooth, leathery, and dark green or greyish above, often slightly hairy beneath, and characteristically have a rather unkempt appearance.

The single or fully double flowers are solitary, or in small clusters of 24, emerging from almost spherical buds in early to mid-summer. Most are intensely fragrant, and nearly all very richly coloured, often velvety, in a range of deep reds, from heavy wine-red through to deep crimsons that shade almost to black. A few are paler in colour, and these include some of the most beautiful pinks.

R. gallica 'Officinalis' bears large, sumptuous, semi-double, and richly scented flowers over several weeks from early to mid-summer, and unless dead headed, will produce a crop of small, oval, brick-red hips which are extremely decorative. *R. gallica* 'Versicolor' has white, pink and light red variegation with a boss of luminous yellow stamens at the centre. It remains one of the best variegated garden roses, although has a tendency to revert to the red-flowered form.

Grafted specimens generally make smaller or more easily confined shrubs and are, therefore, well-suited to smaller gardens. Those on their own rootstocks tend to sucker freely, which makes them useful for hedging.

Cultivation

These robust roses are very cold hardy, and also suitable for warm temperate climates. They require very little special attention, and will tolerate even poor, dry, sandy or calcareous soils, although they will perform best if given a deep, fertile, and moisture-retentive soil, approximately neutral, and enriched with well-rotted organic matter. This group of roses needs very little actual pruning other than to remove weak, spindly branches, dead wood, and very old wood in late winter or very early spring. The removal of old, flowered wood allows light and air to get to the centre of the bush so that new, strong shoots can grow from the base to replace it. Badly placed or over-long shoots can be neatened by cutting them back by approximately one third after the rose has finished flowering.

Rosa gallica 'Officinalis'

'Alain Blanchard'
Vibert, France, 1839   1.2 × 1.2m (4 × 4ft)

The large, velvety blooms are cupped, semi-double and bright crimson, becoming darker and mottled purple with age, making good contrast with golden stamens at the centre. Rich fragrance. Foliage coarse, dark green, dense, on a lax, thorny bush with slender, wiry stems.

ORIGIN: probable cross between *Rosa* × *centifolia* and *Rosa gallica*

'Assemblage des Beautés' ('Rouge Eblouissante')
Probably prior to 1823   1.2 × 0.9m (4 × 3ft)

Of unknown origin, this rose was in cultivation in Angers, France around 1823. The medium-sized flowers are very double, the petals reflexing with maturity to form an almost ball-shaped bloom, with a typical rich *gallica* colour, deep cerise-crimson fading to magenta. An eye-catching rose, strongly perfumed. Bush upright, compact, with almost thornless stems and dark, lush leaves.

'Belle de Crécy'
Prior to 1848   1.2 × 0.9m (4 × 3ft)

This rose, introduced by Roeser in the mid-19th century, is a great beauty, with large, flat blooms, neatly quartered, the central petals crowded around a green eye. The colour is charming – clear, bright pink fading to lilac, lavender and grey. Strongly scented. According to Peter Beales, blooming is not always reliable. An upright bush, rather lax, thornless, with grey-green leaves, the stems arching almost to the ground when in full bloom. G. S. Thomas advises the association of 'Belle de Crécy' with the soft, creamy white of 'Mme Hardy' for good effect.

'Belle Isis'

Parmentier, Belgium, 1845
0.9 × 0.9m (3 × 3ft)

Of unknown parentage, but possibly involving a Centifolia. The creamy buds are almost globose and fleshy; the dainty, fully double flowers are neatly quartered, in a lovely shade of silvery flesh pink seldom seen in a Gallica. Highly scented. Low-growing, somewhat floppy bush, with thorny stems.

'Camaieux'

Vibert, France, 1830
1.2 × 0.9m (4 × 3ft)

A showy rose with semi-double, pale pink blooms striped and splashed with white and red, fading to magenta, then lilac-grey with age, petals clustered around a green eye. Flowers are strongly scented. Compact bush with arching stems.

'Assemblage des Beautés'

'Cardinal de Richelieu'

'Cardinal de Richelieu'
Van Sian, Holland, introduced by Laffay, 1840   1.5 × 1.2m (5 × 4ft)

A sumptuous rose, appreciated for its many-petalled, fully double blooms of deep purple velvet grading through wine-red and
lilac-pink to white at the petal base. When fully open the petals
reflex into a globe. A fine shrub with glossy green shoots, few
thorns, abundant foliage, sometimes rimmed with red-brown.
Pleasing sweet fragrance. Will reward generous feeding, and
especially careful pruning.

'Charles de Mills' ('Bizarre Triomphant')
1.5 × 1.5m (5 × 5ft)

A lovely Gallica of doubtful origin; in some works attributed to
Desportes (1830). Huge, flat blooms perfectly quartered with
many serrated petals arranged around a dark eye. The rich
crimson-magenta fades only slightly to deep red-purple. Lush
foliage on shoots almost free of thorns. Moderately scented.

'Charles de Mills'

'Complicata'

To 3 × 1.8 m (10 × 6ft)

We know little of this extremely charming rose which deserves a place in any informal garden; a Gallica or more probably a cross between a Gallica and *Rosa canina* or *R. macrantha*. The large, single blooms, bright pink with a white eye and numerous golden stamens, are carried along the length of the flexible stems in early summer. There is little scent, but will provide a fine display of hips in autumn. A vigorous, upright, suckering bush, suitable for growing through old apple trees.

'Complicata'

'Cramoisi Picoté'

Vibert, France, 1834

1 × 0.6m (3 × 2ft)

Very pretty and unusual, with small, double blooms, in clusters of 3, the petals strongly reflexing to yield a pompom of frilled, crimson petals, fading to paler, pink-toned crimsons with age. Little or no scent. A slender bush, of neat habit, with small, rounded, dark green leaves.

'D'Aguesseau'

Vibert, France, 1823

1.2 × 0.9m (4 × 3ft)

Very double, flat, quartered blooms with central petals packed around a green eye and outer petals reflexed; vivid crimson, with darker shading at the centre, paler at petal rim. Well-scented. Large, bright green leaves on a vigorous, upright bush.

'Duc de Guiche'
('Sénator Romain')

Prevost, 1835   1.2 × 1.2m (4 × 4ft)

Shapely double blooms, cupped at first, with neatly quartered
petals around a green eye, later reflexing to form a ball, a pleasing magenta-crimson, finely veined purple in warm weather.
Well-scented. Vigorous bush of arching habit, with masses of
dark green leaves.

'Duchesse d'Angoulême'
('Duc d'Angoulême')

Vibert, France, 1835   1 × 1m (3 × 3 ft)

Known as the Wax Rose, referring to the texture of its petals,
probably a cross between a Gallica and Alba, or Centifolia. Pink
buds open to double, shallowly cupped, very fragrant blooms of
a delicate shell pink, with almost translucent petals. Foliage
bright green, the flexible shoots arching with the weight of the
magnificent blooms.

'Duchesse d'Angoulême'

'Duchesse de Montebello'

Laffay, France, 1829   1.2 × 0.9m (4 × 3ft)

One of the loveliest soft pinks, a Gallica-Damask cross, with
small but fully double, fragrant blooms carried relatively early in
summer. A neat and upright bush with abundant, grey-green
foliage. Needs good, fertile soil to give of its best. It is said that
sprays up to 'a yard' long can be cut from lax shoots. It associates well with large, purple-flowered varieties.

'Empress Josephine'

'Empress Josephine' (L'Impératrice Joséphine')

Rosier de Francfort, 1820   1.5 × 1.2m (5 × 4ft)

A precious rose, one of Josephine's collection, first known as
R. × *francofurtana* and re-named later in memory of the Empress.
It is thought to be a cross between a Gallica and R. *pendulina* or
R. *majalis*. The large, loose, semi-double flowers have waved,
rich pink petals with darker veining, and lavender highlights.
Only slightly scented. A low, spreading, and almost thornless
bush with abundant, grey-green leaves. Well-deserving its
renown, a generally healthy shrub often used in cross-breeding.

'Georges Vibert'

Robert, France, 1853   0. 9 × 0.9m (3 × 3ft)

This lovely rose owes its charm to the softly coloured, striped
petals, pale pink, carmine and purple, gently graduated, varying
according to climate, and fading gracefully with age. Blooms
smallish and many-petalled, carried on a neat, upright and
thorny bush with small, dark leaves. Suitable for small gardens.

'Gloire de France' ('Fanny Bias')

Prior to 1819   0.9 × 1.2m (3 × 4ft) or more

The magnificent, tightly quartered blooms reflex to form a pompom of deep pink, shading to soft mauve at petal rims, and
fading almost to white in full sun. Very agreeable fragrance.
A dark-leaved, sprawling bush with few thorns; suitable for
hedges. It is a superb rose, full of charm and should be consid-
erably more widely grown. Some authorities claim that it grows
about 1.2m (4ft) high. Graham Stuart Thomas talks of being
sent this variety under the name of 'Fanny Bias' by Mr Will
Tillotson, of Watsonville, California.

'James Mason'

'Hippolyte' ('Souvenir de Kean')

Early 19th century 1.2 × 1.2m (4 × 4ft)

An ancient rose with pendent clusters of exquisitely shaped, double blooms of rich magenta-purple with paler highlights at the centre; the petals reflex with age to reveal the button eye. Slender but vigorous bush, almost thornless; the branches arch to the ground under the weight of blooms, and are well-clothed in smallish, smooth, dark green leaves. It does not have the normal appearance of a Gallica.

'James Mason'

Peter Beales, Great Britain, 1982 1.5 × 1.2m (5 × 4ft)

A Gallica seedling, dedicated to the English movie star. A captivating rose, with a profusion of scented, almost single flowers, rich bright crimson with darker shading, in contrast to the boss of golden anthers. Early summer. Dense, dark green foliage. Its parents are 'Tuscany Superb' and 'Scarlet Fire'.

'Jenny Duval'

1821 1.2 × 0.9m (4 × 3ft)

No longer widely grown, but with very beautiful, fully double flowers, opening flat, and sometimes quartered, in shades of crimson, mauve, violet and grey-lilac, variable with temperature, situation and age. Exquisite perfume. A tidy, upright bush with grey-green leaves. Often confused with 'Président de Sèze'. The world-famous rosarian Graham Stuart Thomas writes of the flowers and says 'On hot mornings they are frequently of startling magenta-cerise'. Clearly, it is a superb rose that is well worth adding to a garden.

22

'La Belle Sultane' ('Violacea', 'Cumberland', 'Maheka')

18th century   1.5 × 1.2m (5 × 4ft) or more

A very old rose, in cultivation in the gardens at Malmaison.
Large, almost single blooms, with a tuft of golden stamens, are
deep crimson, white at the petal base, fading to violet with age.
Early, short-blooming, well-scented. An almost thornless,
upright bush with long, arching shoots, and sparse, but very
attractive, grey-green leaves.

'Rose des Maures' ('Sissinghurst Castle')

0.9 × 0.9m (3 × 3ft)

An old variety, rediscovered at Sissinghurst by Vita Sackville-
West, and reintroduced in 1947. Remarkable, semi-double
blooms of deep plum-maroon, paler at the edges and on the
reverse, fragrant. A small bush, almost thornless, with a mass of
brittle branches, and thin-textured foliage.

'Tuscany' ('Old Velvet')

Prior to 1820   1 × 0.9m (3 × 3ft) or more

Thought to be the 'Velvet Rose' of Renaissance gardens,
described by Gerard in 1596. The beautiful, flat, semi-double
blooms have a velvety texture, deepest crimson, in fine contrast
with the golden stamens. Little scent and small leaves.
Superseded by its sport 'Tuscany Superb', which has larger
blooms.

'Tuscany Superb'

Rivers, introduced by William Paul, Great Britain, 1848 1.5 × 1.2m (5 × 4ft)

A really superb rose, with more refined, larger, and more
double blooms than 'Tuscany', but always revealing the mass of
conspicuous golden stamens. An upright bush, seen at its best
as a specimen against a green or grey-foliage backdrop.
Intensely scented – a joy in any garden.
ORIGIN: sport of 'Tuscany'

'Tuscany Superb'

DAMASK ROSES

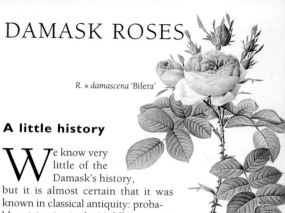

R. × damascena 'Bifera'

A little history

We know very little of the Damask's history, but it is almost certain that it was known in classical antiquity: probably originating in the Middle East, almost certainly grown in Egypt and taken by the Phoenicians from there to the Mediterranean region. With their voluptuous scent and the exquisite form of their flowers, Damasks were without doubt the most commonly grown – on an almost industrial scale – for the pleasure of the ruling classes of Egypt and Rome: whether they were used for coronets or wreaths, to perfume the dining rooms and tables at feasts and banquets, to adorn the statues of the gods, or to be plucked petal by petal into the bath, as Antony and Cleopatra are said to have done. Seductions were also performed amid a sea of petals!

What is known for certain is that this is not a species, but a hybrid in which *Rosa gallica* – closely related to the Damask – is involved. And again we know for certain that two varieties were present in antiquity, two varieties which were to be of paramount importance in later hybridisations when the rose had become the most popular flower in the garden. One was the once-flowering Summer Damask, believed to derive from a cross between the *Rosa gallica* and the Phoenician Rose, *R. phoenicia*. The other is the rose cited by Virgil, the Autumn Damask, or Rose de Quatre Saisons, *R. × damascena* 'Bifera', which blooms a second time in autumn. It is thought to be a hybrid of *R. gallica* with *R. moschata*, the musk rose; this last is unknown in the wild, but has long been cultivated in SW Asia, and around the Mediterranean, for its exotic, musky fragrance. Probable references to Damask roses are found in Pliny the Elder (c. 50AD), and Herodotus, who speaks of a rose with sixty "leaves" growing in Phrygia in the gardens of King Midas. Theophrastus (382–287BC) affirmed the existence of roses with one hundred petals *centifolia* in Latin – and these are presumed to have been Damasks. (Those now known as Centifolias did not arise until the 16th century.)

R × *damascena* was (and still is) the most widely grown for the extraction of attar or otto of rose. The Persian physician Avicenna (980–1037AD), in his *Canon of Medicine*, describes vast areas of arable land in Syria given over to its cultivation. The essence of rose was the basis of many medicines and cosmetics in eastern medicine, and translations of Arabic texts into Latin during the Middle Ages brought its use to many apothecaries in Europe.

Clear references to the Damask appear in the 16th century. One source attributes its introduction to England to Linacre, court physician to Henry VII and Henry VIII, and founder of the Royal College of Physicians. Mattioli confirms its presence in Italy during the same period. And all call it Damask as they are convinced it comes from Damascus. From the 16th century onwards this rose becomes one of the most popular and widely grown, and the discovery of every new variety is greeted with enthusiasm.

Characteristics

The Damasks make shrubs to 2m (6ft) and more in height, with stems densely covered in stout, curved thorns and stiff bristles, bearing light green or grey-green leaves with 5–7 ovate to elliptic leaflets, that are downy beneath. They bear clusters of up to 12 semi- to fully double blooms, often with slightly crumpled and silky petals, which open from (typically) tapering buds, enclosed in long, slender sepals, and give rise to bristly, top-shaped, red hips, unless dead headed. The flowers generally appear in a range of soft, pure colours, usually pinks, and have an unmistakable, rich spicy fragrance. The Autumn Damask, *R.* × *damascena* 'Bifera' is slightly less vigorous, and botanically scarcely distinguishable, other than by its ability to produce a second flush of bloom on the current year's shoots in autumn – the only rose in European gardens to do so prior to the arrival of the China roses in 1792.

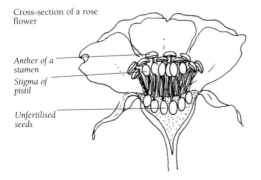

Cross-section of a rose flower

Anther of a stamen

Stigma of pistil

Unfertilised seeds

Unlike the Gallicas, the Damasks do not constitute a homogeneous group: they may be compact or open, more or less thorny, with or without down on the leaves, and some have such slender stems that the flowers are carried in drooping clusters. Apart from the Autumn Damask, they bloom only once at the beginning of summer. Later varieties created in the 19th century, which derive from crosses with other species, such as 'Ispahan', and the Portlands 'Rose de Rescht' and 'Comte de Chambord', were to offer longer or often more continuous blooming seasons.

Cultivation

The Damasks tend to be of lax habit, and in informal plantings may be left to sprawl freely; in more formal gardens, they are sometimes tied-in loosely to cane supports, arranged around the central stem. The flexible stems of the strongest growing lend themselves well to bending over towards the horizontal, espalier-fashion, so that blooms are produced along the length of the stem rather than at the tips only. In each case, they should be planted where the blooms are easily accessible, so as to enjoy their fragrance at close quarters. Damasks require a deep, fertile, and moisture-retentive soil, approximately neutral, and enriched with well-rotted organic matter. In late winter/early spring, cut back main stems by about one third, and shorten the longest laterals (sideshoots). Take out weak, dead or badly placed wood at the same time. Dead heading after flowering is beneficial, cutting back to the nearest full-sized leaves. The Autumn Damask should always be dead headed, and may be cut back a little harder after flowering, followed by application of fertiliser.

'Versicolor'
('York and Lancaster')

. × damascena 'Bifera'

'Belle Amour'

1.8 × 0.9m (6 × 3 ft)

Of unknown origin, and sometimes included with the Albas,
because of its habit and general appearance; it is probably an
Alba–Damask cross. Discovered by Nancy Lindsay in a
monastery garden and introduced in 1940, it attracted attention
because of the unusual, semi-double blooms of soft coral-pink,
with petals almost formally arranged in two ranks, to cup a mass
of rich yellow stamens at the centre. Exotic fragrance of myrrh
with strong notes of anise. Vigorous, thorny bush with beautiful, grey-green leaves.

'Blush Damask'

Prior to 1759   1.2 × 1m (4 × 3ft) or more

Of unknown origin, but a freely suckering, densely twiggy and
prickly bush, indicating that *R. pimpinellifolia*, the Scotch Rose,
is a likely parent. The nodding, well-shaped, highly scented
blooms, produced in great profusion in mid-summer, are
heavy, fully double, blush-pink fading to pale, creamy pink at
the petal edge. Large, sprawling bush with dense foliage. Dead
heading is advisable after blooming. Tolerant of most soil types.
Occasionally, this twiggy shrub is referred to in catalogues and
books as 'Blush Gallica'.

'Botzaris'

1856   1.2 × 0.9m (4 × 3ft)

Deserves to be better known. A tempting rose, creamy white
with a flush of lemon yellow at the centre. The sweet fragrance
is suggestive of an Alba in the parentage. Flowers are very double, flat, often quartered, and with a button eye. A thorny bush
with pale green leaves, needing little, if any, pruning.

'Celsiana'

'Celsiana'
Prior to 1750   1.5 × 1.2m (5 × 4ft)

A very graceful plant, of true Damask character, bearing small clusters of semi-double, richly scented blooms of very soft pink, with silky, almost transparent, crepe de chine petals, which cup a boss of golden stamens. Fades almost white in full sun. A vigorous, dense and upright bush, very free-flowering, with smooth, grey-green leaves.

'Gloire de Guilan'

'Gloire de Guilan'

1.5 × 1.2m (5 × 4ft)

Very ancient. Discovered on the coast of the Caspian Sea by
Nancy Lindsay and introduced to Europe in 1949. It was said to
have been grown in Persia for the production of attar of rose.
The soft pink, very double, often beautifully quartered blooms
open flat, the inner petals gently curving towards the centre.
Very sweet fragrance. Blooms in early summer. A bush of a very
lax habit, with light green foliage and stems densely covered
with small thorns. Best with support.

'Ispahan' ('Pompon des Princes')

Prior to 1832

1.5 × 0.9m (5 × 3ft)

A deserved favourite, appreciated for the long period of bloom
in mid-summer, often the first and last Summer Damask to be
in flower. The blooms are double, arranged in an orderly fashion at first, becoming prettily dishevelled later, with reflexing
petals; they retain their rich pink colour well, and are strongly
perfumed. Fine foliage, small and glossy, on an upright, and
almost thornless, bush.

'La Ville de Bruxelles'

Vibert, France, 1849

1.5 × 1.2m (5 × 4ft)

Magnificent, very large and fully double, quartered blooms with
short central petals and outer petals reflexed, of a bright and
persistent pink. Well-scented. Upright, vigorous, prickly bush,
with arching stems when in full bloom, and abundant and
attractively glossy leaves.

'Ispahan'
('Pompon des Princes')

'Trigintipetala'
('Kazanlik')

'Mme Hardy'

Hardy, France, 1832   1.8 × 1.5m (6 × 5ft)

Monsieur Hardy, gardener to Josephine at Malmaison, may have crossed a Damask with an Alba or Centifolia to obtain this beautiful rose. One of the best loved, and considered the loveliest of white roses, 'Mme Hardy' is the softest of snow-whites. The elegant blooms, cupped at first and opening flat, have inner petals neatly quartered around a green eye, and an intense fruity fragrance, with a hint of lemon. A vigorous shrub with lush, light green leaves and long shoots clothed in a mixture of large and small thorns.

'Mme Zoetmans'

Marest, France, 1830   1.2 × 0.9m (4 × 3ft)

A splendid Damask, similar to Gallica 'Duchesse de Montebello', with large, scented, creamy white blooms, sometimes flushed pink in the middle, revealing a green eye when fully opened. Early flowering. A compact, low-spreading bush.

'Marie Louise'

Prior to 1813   1.2 × 0.9m (4 × 3ft)

One of the roses grown in Empress Josephine's gardens, with beautiful, very large, double, heavy blooms of glowing clear pink, opening flat, later reflexing to form a ball. Sweet and intense perfume. Shrub of compact habit, with few thorns, and abundant, dark green leaves. This rose was raised in Josephine's garden at Malmaison, near Paris, and has the most sumptuous flowers of any rose in this group. Malmaison is situated on the left bank of the Seine and was in beautiful countryside, at that time outside the city walls. Records indicate that a château existed there in 1390.

'Omar Khayyám'

0. 9 × 0.9m (3 × 3ft)

Derives from a plant found on the grave of the poet-translator of
the Rubaiyát, Edward Fitzgerald, in Suffolk, in 1947; it was
originally raised at Kew from seeds taken from a shrub growing
on Omar Khayyám's tomb in Nashapur, in Iran, in 1893. Very
sweetly scented, flat, pale pink and very double blooms are
exquisitely quartered, the petals twisted and folded, the inner-
most curving to form a cushion at the centre. Sometimes bears
malformed flowers. A dense and prickly bush, with small,
downy, grey-green leaves. Useful for small gardens.
Omar Khayyám, who lived from about 1050 to 1123, was a
Persian astronomer and mystic who founded a school of astro-
nomical research in Nashapur. The original rose planted on the
tomb of Edward Fitzgerald at Boulge churchyard, Woodbridge,
Suffolk, died sometime before 1950, but recently fresh plants
raised at Kew Gardens have been established there. It is also
reported that in 1949 buds of the original rose were grafted on
to stocks of *Rosa rugosa* by the long established and well-known
nursery, Notcutt's of Woodbridge.

'St Nicholas'

0.9 × 0.9m (3 × 3ft)

Discovered by Sir Robert James in his Richmond garden in
Yorkshire. An old rose, reintroduced by Hilling in 1950.
Probably a self-sown plant from a Damask and a Gallica cross.
Very pretty, semi-double, pink flowers, fading slowly to white,
with a pronounced golden centre, carried in profusion in early
summer. Dead heading produces a second crop of bloom, and,
if the blooms are not removed, a good crop of orange hips fol-
lows. Low-growing, shrubby little bush, with downy, grey
leaves and fierce thorns.

'Mme Hardy'

'Omar Khayyám'

'Trigintipetala' ('Kazanlik')

1.5 × 1.2m (5 × 4ft) or more

Thought to have been grown extensively in Roman times for the production of attar of rose, and still flourishing in Bulgaria for that purpose. Lovely semi-double, warm pink flowers with soft-textured, gracefully waved petals, and a delicious fragrance that persists on drying; ideal for pot-pourri. A vigorous, upright, but sometimes spreading shrub, perhaps best with support.

'Versicolor' ('York and Lancaster')

1.8 × 1.2m (6 × 5ft)

A rose of charming but unstable colour, with clusters of both deep pink and soft white flowers, sometimes with striped petals. The flowers are loosely double and fragrant, borne on very slender stalks so that they nod under their own weight. The emblem of the House of Tudor following the Wars of the Roses; the white representing the white rose of York, the red, the red rose of Lancaster. A tall, lax, thorny shrub with downy, grey-green leaves. Requires a very fertile soil to grow and flower well.

ALBA
ROSES

A little history

According to one legend, Albas were born of sea-foam, together with Venus; according to another, they were born from her tears. Yet another has it that they are the reflection of the light of heaven. Each is justified; the Albas are amongst the most delicate and sweetly scented of all roses, with the purest of colours.

They are the third in the trinity of most ancient roses, with the Gallicas and Damasks, and are thought to be have been brought to England and Europe by the Romans, although Pliny's descriptions in his *Natural History* do not appear to identify it clearly. Certain acknowledgement comes at the end of the 13th century, when Albertus Magnus and Crescentius both describe the Great Double White. They appear again in the paintings of 15th-century Italy, and, later, in the writings of the father of English botany, William Turner, who dwells on descriptions not only of the typical species (which will subsequently owe its name to Linnaeus) but also other forms, including *R. × alba* 'Maxima', *R. × alba* 'Semi-plena', and *R. × alba* 'Incarnata' ('Maiden's Blush'), then known as the Incarnation Rose. 'Maxima', the Great Double White, was the Jacobite rose of Bonnie Prince Charlie; 'Semi-plena' is said to be the White Rose of York.

Until 1783 the Alba rose was considered a simple species, but examination by eminent botanists of the period revealed it as a hybrid, although its parentage is still disputed. Some regarded it as a cross between *Rosa gallica* with *R. arvensis* or *R. corymbifera*, others suggest *R. canina* and *R. damascena* as parent species. In either case it is now properly known as *Rosa × alba*. From the 16th century onwards, a large number of varieties – few of which have survived to the present day – were cultivated in addition to those which arose spontaneously. The surviving Albas are, for the most part, those created in the 19th century. These long established and cherished roses may be limited in number but they are sufficient to convince us of their undoubted qualities.

33

Characteristics

The Albas are large, long-lived, spreading shrubs with stout, arching stems to 2.5m (8ft) in length, with scattered, hooked thorns. They branch freely to produce dense and substantial bushes with foliage, fruit, and habit that is similar to, but more refined than that of *R. canina*. The abundant leaves comprise 5–7 ovate or rounded leaflets, smooth, and bluish or grey-green above, downy beneath, especially on the leaf veins. The double or semi-double flowers, in clusters of 1–3, are always in shades of white or pink, and are, without exception, beautifully scented. They are carried in spectacular profusion in early to mid-summer. If not dead headed, the single and semi-double forms give rise to large, almost spherical, red hips. Amongst all the roses, the Albas provide one of the finest combinations of foliage, flowers, and fruit. *R. × alba* 'Maxima', almost 2m (6ft) in height, with double, pale pink blooms, fading to cream at the base, is similar to 'Great Maiden's Blush'; *R. × alba* 'Semi-plena', a sport of 'Maxima', is one of the most enchanting, having semi-double, milk-white flowers, in which the central petaloids curl around a golden centre; they are carried amidst an abundance of matt, grey-green leaves. It has an exceptional perfume, and is grown in Bulgaria.

'Céleste'
('Celestial')

Cultivation

Reliably cold-hardy, and disease resistant, they demand little special attention, and thrive even in difficult conditions. They tolerate shade better than any other group of roses, and varying greatly in size, are suited to a range of situations in the garden, from north-facing walls and hedgerows, to the informal shrub or mixed border. They will grow and continue to bloom well with very little pruning other than to remove, dead, weak or badly placed wood. They also respond well if pruned in late winter/early spring; cut back main stems by about one third, and shorten the longest laterals (sideshoots). After flowering, a further tidying and reduction in volume will not do any harm.

R. × alba 'Semi-plena'

'Céleste' ('Celestial')

Prior to 1800

1.5 × 1.2m (5 × 4ft) or more

A heavenly old rose deserving its name, illustrated by Redouté as *R. damascena* 'Aurora'. The elegant, narrow-pointed buds open to large, semi-double, saucer-shaped flowers of clear shell pink, the delicate petals almost translucent. Sweetly scented. Fine, grey-green leaves, with almost thornless, red-tinted stems. Bears elongated hips in autumn. Pierre-Joseph Redouté, a Belgian artist, is often known as the 'Raphael of Flowers', and is famed for his depictions of flowers at Malmaison, near Paris.

35

'Félicité Parmentier'

'Félicité Parmentier'
In cultivation since 1834

1.2 × 0.9m (4 × 3ft)

One of the best Albas, bearing beautifully-shaped, medium-sized flowers, cupped at first and neatly quartered, later reflexing into a ball; white to pale salmon-pink, becoming pale and creamy with age. The buds are tightly-packed with petals. A compact, shrubby and very free-flowering bush, with green stems scattered with dark brown thorns.

'Great Maiden's Blush'
('Cuisse de Nymphe', 'Incarnata', 'La Royale', La Séduisante', 'La Virginale')
Prior to 15th century

2 × 1.5m (6 × 5ft)

A rose with many names, perhaps indicating its enduring popularity. Still very much loved and deservedly so, this exquisite rose is long-lived and very hardy. It bears flat, semi-double blooms of soft, clear blush-pink, with a glorious silky texture, in wreaths along the arching branches, against a backdrop of grey-green leaves. It has a sweet and pure fragrance. Although not remontant it flowers for about a month in mid-summer, and is sturdy enough to form a wild, informal hedge. Distinct from 'Small Maiden's Blush', which has smaller blooms, and seldom reaches more than 1m (3ft) in height. 'Cuisse de Nymphe Emue' is less vigorous, with deeper pink blooms. However, it is not widely grown nor available from nurseries.

'Jeanne d'Arc'
Vibert, France, 1818   1.8 × 1.5m (6 × 5ft)

Resembles 'Maxima', but more compact. The fragrant, double
flowers are a warm creamy shade, and petals are neatly arranged
on opening; they later fade to ivory-white, and as they open
fully, expose a pleasing muddle of petaloids at their centre.
Dark green foliage on a rather twiggy, sprawling shrub. Some
rose authorities claim that this rose is synonymous with
'Angelica minor' and is said to be a dwarf version of the well-
known 'Great Double White'.

'Königin Von Dänemarck'
('Queen of Denmark', 'Belle Courtesan')
1826   2 × 1.2m (6 × 4ft)

A rose of many virtues, created by James Booth in Hamburg,
then in Denmark, hence its German–Danish epithet. The flat-
tish, double blooms are neatly quartered, deep pink at the
centre, with a pretty button eye, fading to pale pink at the edge.
Intense and delicious fragrance. A tall shrub with branches arching to the ground under the weight of bloom, and clothed with
beautiful, grey-green leaves. Suitable for walls, and superb when
climbing into a tree. Good for cutting.
ORIGIN: 'Great Maiden's Blush' seedling × Damask hybrid

'Great Maiden's Blush'
('Cuisse de Nymphe' etc.)

'Mme le Gras de Saint Germain'

Introduced 1846 ⊚ ⊠   2.2 × 1.8m (7 × 6ft) or more

An Alba, or Alba-Damask hybrid, undeservedly neglected
though still available. The strongly scented, double blooms form
an exquisite, regular rosette of ivory-white with a touch of
lemon in the centre. Makes a large, upright shrub, and will
reach 5m (15ft) with support. Sparsely thorny, with grey-green,
downy leaves. Very hardy and a variety that is highly prized and
well worth introducing into a garden.

'Mme Plantier'

'Mme Plantier'

Plantier, France, 1835 ⊚ ⊠ ◈   3.5 × 2.5m (11 × 8ft)

An Alba, possibly crossed with *R. moschata*. The clusters of
many-petalled, flat, and highly scented blooms are creamy
white, fading to pure white, in perfect contrast with the grey-
green foliage. It makes a tall, open shrub, but serves equally well
as a "pillar" or scrambling rose if given support. A favourite of
Vita Sackville-West who grew it at Sissinghurst on old apple
trees, a perfect situation where it may reach 4m (12ft) or more
in height, and spread widely. Sometimes this superb rose is
classified as a Noisette. However, whatever its classification, it is
a rose that is well worth including in a garden, even though it is
large and dominant.

CENTIFOLIA ROSES

A little history

The history of *Rosa × centifolia* is perhaps even more obscure than that of the Gallica and the Damask. It is almost certain that Herodotus' sixty-petal rose was a Damask, and there is no concrete evidence to suggest that ancient civilisations grew the true Centifolias, or that they were present in medieval or Renaissance gardens. Albertus Magnus (1193–1280 AD) leaves among his notes a description which could be that of a Centifolia; other accounts (albeit sketchy) exist from the 16th century and point to the presence of this voluptuous rose in Europe, and to its arrival in England via Austria. It is the French and Dutch, however, who have a special claim to its patronage; it became known, in fact, both as the Rose of Provence, where it was extensively grown, and the Dutch or Holland Rose. The undeserved, derogatory name Cabbage Rose is an unfortunate epithet which comes in at a later date; it refers to the shape rather than the fragrance. The languid and romantic opulence of its blooms was inspirational for painters, above all the Dutch and Flemish, who loved it passionately and painted it at every opportunity (but only after the 17th century); the other name by which this rose is known, in fact, is Rose des Peintres (Painters' Rose).

Cytological studies reveal that the Centifolia is not a species but a rather complex hybrid of at least four roses: *Rosa gallica*, *R. moschata*, the musk rose, *R. phoenicia* and *R. canina*, perhaps with the connivance of the Autumn Damask and an Alba rose. Unlike other old garden roses, *R. × centifolia* was not the result of natural or spontaneous hybridisation but a hybrid produced as a consequence of human intervention, the outcome of a vast genetic mix. The double Centifolias, with their entire reproductive system transformed into a dense cluster of central petaloids, are effectively sterile. Spontaneous variations, therefore, arose only as a result of genetic mutation, and all early varieties arose as sports of the original cross. It was not until the occurrence of a single or semi-double-flowered sport in the early 19th century that the Centifolias could disseminate their genes to create new and different varieties.

The earliest sports were two miniature roses, 'Rose de Meaux', the Dijon Rose, and 'Parvifolia' ('Pompon de Bourgogne') the Burgundy Rose; later came 'Bullata' ('Rose à Feuilles de Laitue'), with crinkled and blistered leaves, and 'Cristata' ('Chapeau de Napoléon') q.v. Another very old mutation, and among the most beautiful, is 'Unique Blanche', the White Rose of Provence, which some tales claim to originate in Suffolk or Norfolk. A variation of great importance was that which gave rise to the Moss roses, with stems clothed in a mass of bristles and thorns of all shapes and sizes, and flower stems and calyces more or less covered with moss-like, glandular growths secreting musky scented oils. The French and the Dutch dedicated themselves to the propagation of many sports from the end of the 16th century onwards. The Centifolias attained perfection in the 18th century, above all as superb cut flowers.

Characteristics

Lax, open and loosely branched shrubs with stems to 2m (6ft) high, clothed in scattered, straight and hooked thorns, and with somewhat coarse, dull green leaves of 5–7 leaflets. Not the most elegant of shrubs, although all is forgiven when the Centifolias open their sumptuous blooms in mid-summer. The scent is so strong and permeating that it can become delightfully intoxicating. Usually double or fully double, their characteristically rounded shape is inevitable, given the profusion of short petaloids at their centre. The blooms are often so heavy, and their stems so slender, that they are unable to carry the opulent blooms upright; since the ample leaves also droop, the shrub takes on the languid appearance that is always affectionately associated with the Centifolias. Some have stems that are weighed to the ground with blooms, and these need support if the flowers are not to be soiled and spoiled. Heavy rain storms are liable to splash soil on flowers borne on low stems.

Cultivation

Cultivation and pruning requirements are as for the Damasks. During the summer the most vigorous Centifolias may produce stems more than one metre (3ft) in length; these should be reduced by a third or even half when dormant so as to prevent them from bending down to ground level when the flowers bloom and create their display.

'Cristata'
('Chapeau de Napoléon')

'Cristata'
('Chapeau de Napoléon')

Vibert, France, 1827   1.5 × 1.2m (5 × 4ft)

Also known as 'Crested Moss' and often classified with the Moss roses. Discovered in 1810 in Fribourg, Switzerland, growing against a convent wall. Amongst the oldest Centifolias, distinguished by the unique crested, moss-like outgrowths on the fleshy sepals, so that the emerging buds resemble a tricorn hat. Blooms open flat, fully double and neatly quartered, highly perfumed and silvery pink. Leaves light green. A highly prized rose and collector's specimen.

'Fantin Latour'

c. 1900   1.5 × 1.2m (5 × 4ft)

A distinctive rose much grown for exhibition, and deserving of its many awards. Although classified with the Centifolias, its foliage is suggestive of China rose parentage. Named for Henri Fantin-Latour (1836–1904) well-known for his flower portraits, including many roses such as this. The deliciously scented blooms are a clear and delicate pink, darker in bud, and paler with age, cup-shaped when fully open and with reflexing outer petals. A large, almost thornless shrub, with smooth, dark, glossy leaves and rounded leaflets.

'Fantin Latour'

'Juno'

Laffay, France, 1832 1.5 × 1.2m (5 × 4ft)

A classic Centifolia with very double, globular flowers, eventual-ly opening flat to reveal a button eye at the centre; strongly scented, blush-pink. A lax, sprawling bush with gracefully arch-ing branches needing support when in bloom. It is ideal for trailing over a low wall. Light green leaves.

ORIGIN: *Rosa gallica* × a China Rose

'Petite de Hollande' ('Pompon des Dames')

Raised in Holland, c. 1800 1.2 × 0.9m (4 × 3ft)

A compact, miniature Centifolia eminently suitable for smaller gardens. The highly scented, fully double flowers are crowded with clear pink petals, shaded with darker pink towards the centre, slightly bigger than those of 'Rose de Meaux' and carried in attractive clusters.

'Parvifolia' ('Pompon de Bourgogne')

Prior to 1664 0. 8 × 0.6m (32 × 24in)

The Burgundy Rose is one of the smallest and oldest of Centifolias. The deliciously scented flowers, 2.5cm (1in) across, are fully double pompoms, rich pink shaded with lavender, and paler in the middle. Compact, upright, and twiggy, with few thorns and well-clothed with small dark leaves. Given full sun, a prolific bloomer, suited to terrace and patio plantings. It is probably of Gallica origin. Records indicate that there are two forms of this rose, one taller than the other as well as being larger in its parts. Both have been cultivated in Britain since the eighteenth century.

'Reine des Centfeuilles'

Belgium, 1824 — 1.5 × 0.9m (5 × 3ft)

Once famous, this free-flowering rose much deserves a revival. The superb blooms look almost as though they have been trimmed flat; large, neatly quartered even when fully open, deep pink and very fragrant. A distinctive, large-leaved shrub which reveals an open habit.

'Rose de Meaux' ('De Meaux', 'Pomponia')

Prior to 1789 — 60 × 60cm (2 × 2ft)

Dedicated to Dominique Séguier, Bishop of Meaux, a great lover of roses. A miniature, with fully double, pompon-form blooms to 4cm (1½in) across, in a clear pink that is typical of the Centifolias. A shrubby, compact and upright bush, with tiny, bright green leaves. 'White de Meaux' (1637) has white flowers.

'Rose de Meaux'
('De Meaux', 'Pomponia')

'Spong'

Spong, Great Britain, 1805 — 0.9 × 0.9m (3 × 3ft)

Named for the gardener who raised it, a dwarf Centifolia, taller than 'Rose de Meaux' and with wider, fully double blooms, cup-shaped at first, later flat, deep pink, darker at the centre, paler at the rim. Early and long-flowering, a compact, unbranched shrub with plentiful, grey-green leaves. Dead flowers must be removed as soon as they fade; if left on the shrub they soon look extremely unsightly and mar the entire plant's appearance.

43

'Tour de Malakoff'

Soupert & Notting, Luxembourg, 1856   2.5 × 1.5m (8 × 5ft)

Remarkable in bloom, the loosely double flowers are very large, peony-like, and of a papery texture; magenta, veined violet, fading to grey-mauve, and with a paler reverse, they open flat to reveal shining stamens at the centre. Scented. A vigorous, rather sprawling shrub with small, smooth leaves, and long shoots that need support. Can be grown as a climber. Needs fertile soil to ensure that it blooms well.

ORIGIN: *Rosa gallica* × a China Rose

'Unique Blanche'
('Unique', 'White Provence', 'Vierge de Cléry')

Needham, Suffolk, 1775   1.5 × 1.2m (5 × 4ft)

An exquisite rose with superb blooms opening from long, elegant, red-tinted buds; cupped, double, with delicate, silky white petals, creamy within the folds, arranged around a button eye. A vigorous and very beautiful shrub deserving a place in any garden, in good soil. Gives its best in dry summers, its only fault being that it tends to ball in wet weather. Although discovered more than two-hundred years ago in an English village, it is, like so many old and cherished roses, still available for sale through specialist rose nurseries. These roses have a nostalgic quality that creates thoughts of quiet, country gardens.

MOSS ROSES

A little history

One of the most curious mutations in roses is that which produced the Moss roses. Sports of the Centifolias and Damasks, they have a firm, dense, moss-like growth on the calyces and sometimes on the flower stems, which bears glandular tissue that secretes heavily scented oils quite separately from the heady fragrance produced by the flowers.

The Moss rose is recorded for the first time in 1696, while Philip Miller, Curator of the Chelsea Physic Garden, states that he saw a specimen in the Leyden Botanic Garden in 1727, and manages to acquire one for Chelsea soon afterwards, describing it as *Rosa muscosa*. This was the original mossy sport from *R. centifolia*, now known as *Rosa centifolia* 'Muscosa', the Common Moss, Old Moss, or Old Pink Moss, although Peter Beales suggests that this last name refers to different types of Moss roses grown later, in the 19th century, neater and more compact, but of a more tender disposition. In any event, from the end of the 18th century other forms and colours began to emerge, such as 'Muscosa Alba' ('Shailer's White Moss' or 'White Bath'), the Blush Moss, 'Muscosa Incarnata', and the Striped Moss, 'Muscosa Striata' ('Oeillet Panaché'), with many other variations whose origins are little known. In the beginning of the 19th century a single-flowered Centifolia Moss occurred, allowing the breeding of hundreds of Moss roses. The Moss roses which have survived to the present day, however, are not very widely grown in comparison with other groups, although it does them an injustice to regard them merely as collector's curiosities. They have great charm.

Characteristics and cultivation

Most are rather lax shrubs having in common the typical mossy covering, sometimes covering stems and calyces, in other cases just the calyx. On Mosses derived from the Damasks, the moss is usually stiffer, and brown in colour. They vary in size from tiny shrubs like 'Mousseline' to those suitable for rose pillars, such as 'Jeanne de Montfort'. Those that flower only once often have a long period of bloom, and some are remontant, or repeat-flowering. Graham Stuart Thomas recommends the older varieties, the original Moss roses such as 'Muscosa' or 'Muscosa Alba', rather than the hybrids created later, even though one can also find roses of great beauty, such as the well-known and widely acclaimed 'Comtesse de Murinais', among the latter.

More robust and erect than the Centifolia, they have the same characteristics and needs and should be treated in the same way. If it is necessary to keep them compact, they can be cut back by up to half in late winter/early spring.

'Alfred de Dalmas'

Laffay, France, 1855   1.2 × 0.9m (4 × 3ft)

Often regarded as synonymous with 'Mousseline'; many authors consider them two different varieties. Clusters of smallish, semi-double blooms, are creamy with a delicate pink flush, later fading to white, carried in early summer, and in several lesser flushes until autumn. The fragrance is reminiscent of honey-suckle and sweet peas – a superb rose for a scented garden. A very thorny, lax shrub, not very mossed.

'Blanche Moreau'

Moreau-Robert, France, 1880   1.2 × 0.9m (4 × 3ft) or more

A Damask-Moss with pure white blooms contrasting beautifully with the purplish-black thorns and dark, bristly moss: cup-shaped, medium-sized, very double and sweetly scented, with a green eye. Slightly remontant. A vigorous, spreading shrub with slender stems.

ORIGIN: 'White Quatre Saisons' × 'Comtesse de Murinais'

'Comtesse de Murinais'

Vibert, France, 1843   2.2 × 1.5m (7 × 5ft)

A Damask-Moss with flat, very double, and exquisitely fragrant flowers, soft pink paling to creamy white with age. Dark moss is plentiful and highly aromatic. A tall and vigorous shrub, the conspicuously veined leaves revealing its Damask parentage. It is, without doubt, a superb rose and one that has been used to breed several other Moss-types. For example, the superb 'Blanche Moreau' (detailed above) owes part of its parentage to 'Comtesse de Murinais'.

'Comtesse de Murinais'

'Dresden Doll'

Ralph Moore, USA, 1975 25 × 15cm (10 × 6in)

A Miniature Moss with delightful, cup-shaped, semi-double
blooms; soft pink and scented. Heavy moss on buds and stems;
leathery, glossy bright green leaves. Ideal as a patio or pot rose.
ORIGIN: 'Fairy Moss' × un-named Moss seedling

'Duchesse de Verneuil'

Portemer, France, 1856 1.5 × 0.9m (5 × 3ft)

The most sophisticated of Damask-Mosses, which owes its
elegance and delicacy to a probable cross with a China Rose.
Camellia-like flowers are flat with many curving petals, bright
pink, shading almost to salmon-pink in the petal folds. It has a
rich, sweet scent. Dense, dark green moss is offset well against
light green leaves.

'Eugénie Guinoisseau'

B. Guinoisseau, France, 1864 1.8 × 1.2m (6 × 4ft)

Large, cup-shaped, and beautifully scented blooms of a very
interesting colour, cerise with purple-violet, ageing to maroon.
Remontant in a good season. Dark green moss and smooth
leaves. Best with support. It is an excellent rose as it creates a
profusion of blooms throughout summer and into autumn.
This quality, combined with its beautiful colouring, makes it a
desirable feature in a garden.

'Eugénie Guinoisseau'

'Général Kléber'
Robert, France, 1856 1.5 × 1.2m (5 × 4ft)

A very fine Damask-Moss. Blooms large, double, scented, open-ing flat and quartered, showing a button eye surrounded by small wavy petals; soft, glowing pink, shaded mauve. A dense, upright shrub with buds covered in a thick reddish-green moss, almost thornless stems, and abundant fresh green leaves. Should be more widely grown.

'Gloire des Mousseux' ('Mme Alboni')
Laffay, France, 1852 21.5 × 0.9m (5 × 3ft)

A Damask-Moss with small clusters of exceptionally large blooms, strongly and sweetly scented, the numerous, almost translucent, inner petals neatly overlapping, the outer reflexing. Soft, glowing pink, fading with age. An upright bush with reddish-brown moss, and bright green leaves.

'James Mitchell'
E. Verdier, France, 1861 1.5 × 1.2m (5 × 4ft)

Damask-Moss with dainty buds clothed in dark green-brown moss, opening to rounded, double blooms, later becoming flat, magenta fading to lilac-pink. Highly scented and free-flowering. A tidy and graceful shrub with pleated, bronze-flushed leaves.

'Général Kléber'

'Japonica' ('Moussu du Japon') 🌱 🏺

1.2 × 0.9m (4 × 3ft)

The most densely mossed of all roses; stems, buds, stalks and parts of the leaves are clothed in dark green, aromatic moss. The flowers are less double than most Mosses, rather loose and slightly untidy, magenta ageing lilac-pink. Scented. A lax and low-growing shrub, with dark metallic leaves. Slow to establish but then vigorous.

'Jeanne de Montfort' 🌱

Robert, France, 1851

2.5 × 1.5m (8 × 5ft)

A vigorous, tall-growing shrub, one of the largest of the Mosses, with large clusters of very fragrant, flat, semi-double flowers: soft pink with silvery petal rims, and a tuft of golden stamens at the centre. Very mossy buds and emerald green foliage. Occasionally it has a remontant nature.

'Japonica'
('Moussu du Japon')

'Maréchal Davoust'

Robert, France, 1853 1.2 × 0.9m (4 × 3ft)

A tidy Damask-Moss with unusual flowers in shades of pink, red and carmine shaded with purple, lilac and grey. Double and shallowly cupped, reflexing when fully open to expose a green eye surrounded by short, curled petaloids. The colour lasts well; very free-flowering, with dark brown moss, and an attractive covering of grey-green leaves.

'Muscosa'

1.5 × 1.2m (5 × 4ft)

R. × *centifolia* 'Muscosa', the Common Moss or Old Moss, appeared in France at the end of the 17th century, and is still one of the best Mosses in cultivation. The very double, cup-shaped and flat-topped blooms are strongly scented, clear pale pink, emerging from buds well-covered in green moss. They are carried over a period of about two months in summer. A vigorous shrub of open habit.

'Nuits de Young'

Laffay, France, 1845 1.2 × 0.9m (4 × 3ft)

A famous and very reliable Moss, and unique amongst Old Roses for the depth of colour in its velvety, purple-maroon flowers, which, when fully open, display a few shining stamens. Moss is dark but not profuse, leaves small and dark green. A compact, upright, and suckering shrub.

'Salet'

Lacharme, France, 1854 1.5 × 1.2m (5 × 4ft)

An Autumn Damask-Moss hybrid, and amongst the most reliable of repeat-flowering Mosses. Large, deep pink blooms, double, and flat when fully open, with narrow, untidily quartered petals. A vigorous shrub with few thorns and bright green leaves, especially on emergence.

'Soupert et Notting'

Pernet Père, France, 1874 1 × 0.6m (3 × 2ft)

A pleasing Autumn Damask-Moss with neat, globular blooms with well-ordered petals of deep pink, fading to pale pink at the outer edge. Strongly scented and remontant with greenish-brown moss. Part of the appeal of this Moss rose is its ability to continue flowering well into autumn. Also, its size makes it suitable for planting in a small garden.

'Salet'

'William Lobb' ('Old Velvet Moss', 'Duchesse d'Istriche')

Laffay, France, 1855   2.2 × 1.8m (7 × 6ft)

A Damask-Moss with clusters of ample, semi-double flowers with muddled centres; crimson-purple, fading to lavender-grey, petals with a lilac-pink reverse. Buds well-covered in green moss, both moss and flowers very strongly scented. A tall and thorny shrub, best with support for the long shoots which bend under the weight of bloom.

'Zoe'

Vibert, France, 1830   1.2 × 0.9m (4 × 3ft)

Bears neat and charming rosettes of many narrow, fluted petals around a small, green button eye. The scented flowers are small, and in many shades of pink. Densely clothed in aromatic, purple-brown moss. Vigorous shrub with many slender thorns, and mid-green leaves.

'Zoe'

CHINA
ROSES

A little history

Western China is perhaps the most important centre of diversity for the genus *Rosa*, and it is clear that they inspired the same enthusiasm and passion in China that they were later to provoke in the West; Confucius had in his library some 600 volumes on their cultivation. Whilst the history of how this immense natural heritage was exploited in their native regions remains to be unravelled, the consequence of their arrival in Europe in 1752, when 'Old Blush' was sent to Sweden by Peter Osbeck, was clearly to be of immense importance. It was the spark which eventually triggered off a revolution whose effects are still apparent in gardens today.

Rosa chinensis

Until the arrival of the China roses, roses grown in European gardens belonged to a small number of interrelated groups: the Gallicas, Damasks, Albas and Centifolias, and their mossy sports. From the beginning of the 19th century, roses underwent a complete transformation by means of gradual, continuous manipulation to yield a vast array of very different varieties. China roses brought with them an extremely precious genetic component, that previously was present only in the Autumn Damask; the gene for remontancy, the ability to bear two or more flushes of bloom during the season. All the rest bloomed once only, the latter bloomed again in the autumn. The China roses, on the other hand, began flowering in early summer, and continued to do so on each flush of new shoots until autumn. It is for this reason that 'Old Blush', also known as 'Parson's Pink China', was additionally called the Monthly Rose.

Moreover, China roses have glossy leaves with an almost metallic sheen, in contrast to the dull surfaces of the Gallicas, Damasks and Albas, and their reds are also markedly different; fresh, light lacquer-reds as against the more sanguine, blue-toned reds of Western roses. Even their scents are of a different class; light and fruity as opposed to sweet, heavy, penetrating and intoxicating.

52

There are two Chinese species whose genetic complement was of seminal importance in the development of the new roses. *Rosa chinensis* (syn. *R. indica*), the China Rose or Bengal Rose, an evergreen shrub of variable habit from dwarf to semi-climbing, with single or semi-double flowers of pale pink, scarlet or crimson, repeat-flowering, with smooth, fragile stems, and small elegant leaves; and *R. gigantea,* a slightly tender, evergreen or semi-evergreen climber, reaching up to 15m (50ft), with large, creamy flowers to 15cm (6in) across, having a distinctive fragrance, likened by the imaginative to fresh China tea leaves. It blooms profusely in early summer, followed by other less abundant flushes. The hybrid of the two, *R. × odorata*, the Tea Rose, with single or double blooms in shades of white, pale pink, or pale yellow, was to open still further chapters.

There is little documentary evidence of these Chinese species in Europe prior to the 19th century, although as Graham Stuart Thomas notes, Bronzino seems to have painted them during the Renaissance, and three Chinese species appear in the herbarium of one of the pupils of Linnaeus. Perhaps introduced by some traveller from India, their potential was unrecognised, and it was many more years before they became common.

The great breakthrough came not from the true species, but from four varieties which the geneticist Hurst defines as "stud roses". His cytological studies revealed much information about the history of the rose, and especially of China roses. These four plants arrived on the vessels of the East India Company, the first reaching London at the end of the 18th century. The 'Old Blush' or 'Parson's Pink China', derived

Rosa gigantea

from *R. chinensis,* with pink blooms, which was introduced from Canton in 1789 by Sir Joseph Banks, then honorary director at Kew. 'Slater's Crimson China' (*R. chinensis* 'Semperflorens'), which came from a garden in Calcutta, was given in 1792 to Gilbert Slater, director of the East India Company, who tended it in his greenhouse.

The other two were also hybrids – this time derived from *R. × odorata* – which arrived in 1809 and 1824. 'Hume's Blush' tea-scented China, which came from a nursery in Canton, was brought by an agent of the British East India Company, and received in London by Sir Abraham Hume. In the same year (1809), despite the Revolutionary and Napoleonic Wars, it sailed with a permit of safe conduct to Josephine at Malmaison: a plant with semi-double blooms ranging from ivory to pink and the typical tea-rose fragrance. 'Park's Yellow' tea-scented China was imported by John Dampier Parks, who collected plants in China on behalf of the Royal Horticultural Society; a plant with large, double blooms, pale sulphur yellow, again with the unusual scent of tea. Although neither are now in cultivation in Europe, their offspring survive.

From the early 19th century onward, the genes of the stud roses were incorporated into all the new roses produced from calculated hybridisations by a growing breed of professional nurserymen, yielding those groups of roses which were dominant in the gardens of the last century; the Portlands, Bourbons, Noisettes, Tea roses and Hybrid Perpetuals. Many of these are still with us today, irreplaceable and loved above all because they have a grace and beauty unrivalled in their modern counterparts.

Quite aside from their historical significance, once their elegance and grace had been recognised, it was inevitable that the Chinese species and their simple hybrids would take their place in the nurseryman's catalogues, thus finding their way into gardens beside the Western roses and their new semi-Chinese cousins born from the recent hybridisations, but, given their characteristics, with quite different garden use.

Characteristics and cultivation

China roses are small, slender, airy and twiggy shrubs, occasionally climbers, with elegant, dainty, and glossy foliage. They bear relatively small, fragrant, semi-double or double flowers in a delicate range of pinks, with a few crimsons or flame reds, from early summer continuously through until autumn, or in milder climates, until winter. Eminently suitable for smaller gardens, they are best grown in groups of three or more, to create soft graduations of tone and colour; the refinement of their colour range and their compactness is also useful in bedding, for situations where the loud and exuberant

'Cécile Brunner'

colours of the modern roses would be inappropriate. They need little pruning other than to remove dead wood, and to tidy badly placed growth in late winter. As with other continuously blooming roses, they need a fertile soil, and will benefit from feeding with a general rose fertiliser in early spring, and again following the first flush of bloom. They must have a position in full sun to give of their best.

'Cécile Brunner'

Veuve-Ducher, introduced by J. Pernet-Ducher, 1881   90 × 60cm (3 × 2ft)

A miniature hybrid of the *chinensis* type, perhaps not correctly classified here with the Chinas, and often included with the Dwarf Polyanthas. An extremely pretty and dainty rose which, together with 'Perle d'Or' played an important role in development of the Miniatures. Blooms are silvery blush-pink, darker at the centre, and of perfect shape, like a tiny Tea rose. Seldom out of flower, and well-scented. A very low-growing bush with few thorns, and small, dark green leaves. Invaluable for cutting. The climbing sport 'Climbing Cécile Brunner' which reaches 6m (20ft) in good conditions, was produced in California in 1884. 'Cécile Brunner, White', introduced by Fanque in France, in 1909, is a white-bloomed variety with a delicate and attractive hint of peach, lemon, and buff.

ORIGIN: Seedling Poly-pom × Tea Rose 'Mme de Tartas' or 'Souvenir d'un Ami'

'Cramoisi Supérieur'
('Agrippina')

'Comtesse du Cayla'

P. Guillot, France, 1902 90 × 90cm (3 × 3ft)

Almost single, flat, intensely scented blooms, with the typical
Tea rose fragrance, open as gracefully and ephemerally as a wild
rose. The bush, however, blooms regularly throughout summer,
each flower a glowing coral pink, tinted with copper, gold and
soft orange. Of very open and slender growth with sparse, delicate leaves that are purple-tinted when young.

'Cramoisi Supérieur'
('Agrippina')
Coquereau, France, 1832 90 × 60cm (3 × 2ft)

The small, dainty, cupped, semi-double blooms of crimson-red
are slightly nodding, and have very little scent. The bright and
unfading colour, and its reliably long flowering season, are the
reasons that its introduction was highly praised; it was regarded
by some as a replacement for 'Slater's Crimson China'. A compact and slender bush, with neatly toothed leaves. The climbing
form was introduced by Couturier, France, in 1885; to 3m
(10ft) high, it deserves more attention. Both forms need a warm,
sunny site to bloom well. 'Cramoisi Supérieur' forms an ideal
shrub for planting in a small garden and at the side of a patio.

'Fabvier'
Laffay, France, 1832 90 × 60cm (3 × 2ft)

A China rose close to a Floribunda and suitable for bedding. It
bears large clusters of double, bright crimson-scarlet flowers,
occasionally flecked with white, enhanced by the glossy, dark
green leaves. Compact, tidy bush, with a long flowering season.
It is a superb bedding rose.

'Fellemberg'
('La Belle Marseillaise')

Prior to 1837, introduced by Fellemberg, Germany, 1857   2 × 2m (6 × 6ft)

A valuable rose for the cascading trusses of cerise-crimson
blooms; double, cup-shaped at first and dishevelled later, with
long, pointed petals. A vigorous, spreading shrub, more thorny
than most Chinas, with lush, mid-green leaves; flowering from
summer to autumn. May be trained as a pillar rose. It is an
amazingly free-flowering variety and widely considered to be
worth planting, especially in a small garden.

'Gloire des Rosomanes'
('Ragged Robin')

Vibert, France, 1825   1.5 × 1.2m (5 × 4ft)

A China-Bourbon hybrid, much used in the past as understock,
especially in the USA, and in the breeding of many Hybrid
Perpetuals. Rather large, semi-double blooms, bright cerise,
sweetly scented and in large trusses, carried continuously
throughout summer to autumn. A vigorous bush, sometimes
used for hedging in Mediterranean climates.

'Grüss an Teplitz'

Geschwind, Hungary, introduced by Lambert in 1897   2 × 1.2m (6 × 4ft)

A China-Bourbon hybrid, with intense, spicy fragrance, producing both small and large trusses of flat, fully double flowers on
short, slender stalks: rich crimson becoming darker with age.
Robust and sturdy in growth, and generous in bloom, from
summer to autumn. Suitable for hedging, and as a climber if
given the support of wall, trellis or pergola, when it may reach
3–4m (10–12ft). The complexity of its parentage makes it difficult to slot this variety into any group. Often, it is simply placed
among shrub roses.
ORIGIN: ('Sir Joseph Paxton' × 'Fellemberg') × ('Papa Gontier' ×
'Gloire des Rosomanes')

'Fabvier'

'Hermosa'
('Armosa')

Marcheseau, France, 1840   90 × 60cm (3 × 2ft)

A compact, bushy China with small, cupped, fully double flowers of the softest pink, set against bluish-green leaves. Very agreeably scented, and prolific blooming. Four different rose breeders between 1834 and 1841 produced seedling plants which were known as China-reversions and resembled the one now known as 'Hermosa'. Indeed this variety has had at least four names in addition to 'Hermosa'. In some books it is classified as a Bourbon, but whatever its derivation it is certainly an excellent small shrub. 'Hermosa' is readily available and widely recommended for its hardiness.

'Irène Watts'

Guillot, France, 1896   60 × 60cm (2 × 2ft)

Pretty, apricot-tinted buds open to small, graceful, flat and loosely double blooms of soft peach-pink, flushed salmon, fading white and opening to reveal a button eye. A dwarf bush with dark green leaves edged purplish-brown. Continuous flowering throughout summer. Hardy.

'Le Vésuve'
('Lemesle')

Laffay, France, 1825   90 × 90cm (3 × 3ft)

The pointed buds open to large, nodding, loosely double and somewhat blowsy blooms of silvery pink, shaded deeper pink at the centre, and becoming darker with age. Well-scented, and blooming generously until autumn. A densely branched and thorny shrub, needing full sun and a warm site to give of its best; it is suitable for growing under glass, and would thrive in a large conservatory.

'Mutabilis'
('Tipo Ideale')
        1.5 × 1.5m (5 × 5ft)

An old rose of uncertain origin. Introduced to Europe in 1896, when a specimen was given to the Swiss botanist Henri Correvon of Geneva, by Prince Ghilberto Borromeo. A surprising specimen of independent character, occasionally growing to 2.5m (8ft) or more in favourable soils, sites and climates. The elegant, flame-coloured buds open to single, buff-yellow flowers, later darkening to pink and crimson, in a manner which reveals its wild Chinese ancestry. It is a graceful and exceptionally elegant shrub, with wiry, purple-tinted stems and small, glossy, evergreen leaves, bronzed when young; it bears a profusion of flowers recurrently throughout the season, and in mild seasons may bloom until Christmas. Best in a warm, sunny position but is tolerant of semi-shade in warmer areas. It has the advantage of being a long-lived shrub.

'Mutabilis'
('Tipo Ideale')

'Old Blush'
('Parson's Pink China')

1.5 × 1.2m (5 × 4ft)

This rose is probably 'Parson's Pink China', grown since the 10th century in China, and brought to England from Canton, in 1789 by Sir Joseph Banks. 'Old Blush' is almost certainly the rose sent to Linnaeus in Sweden by his pupil Peter Osbeck in 1752. It has an exceptionally long flowering period, from spring to winter in a good season, and bears smallish, cupped, double blooms of soft silvery pink with darker shading. It has a fragrance reminiscent of sweet peas. Upright, twiggy shrub, with very few thorns; notably strong and healthy, and easy to grow. Will reach 3m (10ft) if grown against a wall, and perhaps higher when given a position against one in full sun.

'Old Blush'
('Parson's Pink China')

'Perle d'Or'
Rambaud, introduced by Dubreuil, 1884   1.2 × 0.8m (4 × 2½ft)

Bears clusters of beautifully shaped, very sweetly scented double
flowers of soft apricot-pink, flushed with buff and gold, fading
to creamy buff. Reliably recurrent. A dense, twiggy and almost
thornless bush with ample, soft green leaves. Usually remains
compact, but may reach 2m (6ft) in good conditions.
ORIGIN: *R. × multiflora* × 'Mme Falcot'

'Perle d'Or'

'Rouletii'
30 × 30cm (12 × 12in)

A Miniature discovered by Dr Roulet in a Swiss village, growing
there as a pot plant, and sent to Henri Correvon in Geneva, who
introduced it in 1922. Its provenance is obscure; Graham Stuart
Thomas believes it to be a mutant of *Rosa chinensis* 'Pumila'. It
was the parent of many Miniature roses. Bears small, fully double flowers in erect clusters, deep pink, and carried over long
periods in summer. A graceful, hardy and resilient little bush,
with very glossy, semi-evergreen leaves; dense and stems well-
armed with thorns.

'Viridiflora'
(*Rosa chinensis* 'Viridiflora', 'Rosa Verde')
Prior to 1845   90 × 90cm (3 × 3ft)

The Green Rose is a monstrous sport, possibly derived from
R. chinensis 'Pallida'. Known prior to 1845, it cannot be considered a beauty by any stretch of the imagination. The petals are
reduced to clusters of green scales, streaked red or purple; it
dries well for winter arrangements. Additionally, it is much in
demand by flower arrangers for display in summer. A strong,
healthy bush, very easy to grow.

PORTLAND
ROSES

A little history

At the end of the 18th century, a shrub which was to play an important role in the great evolutionary mosaic of the rose made its appearance in Europe: the Portland Rose. Margaret Cavendish Bentinck, the Duchess of Portland, is usually credited with its discovery, c. 1780, in the famous nursery at Paestum, near Naples. She introduced it to England, and later sent cuttings to France. It was André Dupont, Director of the Luxembourg Gardens in Paris, who christened it in honour of its discoverer, 'Duchess of Portland'. It is a repeat-flowering, single rose of intense, clear pink to red whose parents have been identified as *Rosa gallica* 'Officinalis' and the Autumn Damask; some also suggest the involvement of a China rose, possibly 'Slater's Crimson' China. Given the dates, this seems unlikely.

Gardeners and enthusiasts, always receptive to novelty, were immediately interested in the Portland Rose, and among them was Count Lelieur, Director of the Imperial Gardens. It is to him that we owe one of the first of a series of crosses, the Lelieur Rose, later called 'Rose du Roi', a Portland-China cross of 1815, which was important in the later rise of the Hybrid Perpetuals. 'Rose du Roi' was considered the leading member of the entire group of Portland roses, a group which never became very numerous, even though some 84 varieties were growing at Kew in 1848. They were not very fertile, and somewhat reticent as subjects for hybridisation. Some of them, however, such as 'Comte de Chambourd' and 'Rose de Rescht' have met with enormous favour, and are still grown today.

Characteristics and cultivation

Portland roses have inherited from their Gallica parents the erect bearing of the blooms, usually carried well clear of the foliage, although they are generally shorter shrubs, more compact in habit. The influence of the Damasks is apparent in their fragrance. The Portlands are generally considered to have much in common with the older roses in terms of flower form, foliage and fragrance, with the additional advantage of repeat-flowering. Since most are of quite small stature, they are invaluable in the mixed borders of smaller gardens. Grow in fertile soil, in sun, and feed with a general rose fertiliser in early spring, and again after the first flush of bloom. They should be dead headed after flowering. Remove dead, weak and very old growth, and prune strong stems back by one half to one third in late winter.

'Arthur de Sansal'

Cartier, France, 1855   90 × 60cm (3 × 2ft)

Tidy, very double, rosette-shaped blooms of deep purplish-crimson, paler on the petal reverse, quartered, and with a button eye. Well-scented, with a long flowering season from mid-summer. A vigorous small shrub, with abundant, light green foliage, but susceptible to mildew. It is a hybrid of 'Géant des Batailles' and forms a sturdy plant.

'Blanc de Vibert'

Vibert, France, 1847   90 × 90cm (3 × 3ft)

A lovely rose with cupped, fully double blooms, white, tinted with lemon at the centre. Highly perfumed and recurrent. An upright bush with ample, light green, Gallica-like leaves.

'Comte de Chambord'

Moreau-Robert, France, 1860   90 × 60cm (3 × 2ft)

Amongst the most renowned of Portland roses, it remains a treasure which competes with the best. The large, rich lilac-pink blooms are cupped at first, later opening flat and quartered, with the outer petals paler and reflexing. It blooms with a strong flush from mid-summer, intermittently until autumn, and has a strong, heady fragrance. A stout shrub, with plentiful dark green leaves, and strong shoots which arch with the weight of blooms. Ideal for small gardens and mixed borders. Many rose authorities are convinced that this is the best Portland rose still in cultivation, attributing this to its Gallica flower shape and perpetual-flowering nature.

'Jacques Cartier'

Moreau-Robert, France, 1868   90 × 60cm (3 × 2ft)

A Portland-China hybrid, very similar to, but not as generous as 'Comte de Chambord'; the blooms have a pleasing rosette form, very flat and with shorter petals at the centre: pearly pink, darker in the middle, and slightly muddled with maturity. Delightful scent and dark green leaves. This rose is named after the French navigator and explorer Jacques Cartier (1491–1557) who on his second voyage in 1536 sailed up the St Lawrence. He made further voyages to what later became French Canada.

'Jacques Cartier'

'Mme Knorr'

V. Verdier, France, 1855   90 × 90cm (3 × 3ft)

Slightly more substantial than most Portlands, with large, semi-double flowers of bright rose-pink, with a paler petal reverse, and an intense fragrance. Strong shrub with a habit of growth resembling 'Comte de Chambord' and 'Jacques Cartier', but with fewer leaves.

'Portland Rose' ('Duchess of Portland')

c. 1790   90 × 60cm (3 × 2ft)

A spectacular rose when in full bloom, bearing numerous fragrant, semi-double, cerise-crimson flowers with prominent golden stamens, in summer and again in autumn. Needs deadheading. A short, bushy shrub with fine foliage.

'Rose de Rescht'

90 × 60cm (3 × 2ft)

An ancient rose discovered in Persia, in 1940, by Nancy Lindsay, growing in a garden in the town of Rescht. It has Gallica-like foliage, and Damask characteristics in its short stems and strong fragrance, and is sometimes included with the Damasks. It bears small, tight rosettes, almost pompom-form, in large, upright clusters amidst luxuriant emerald green foliage. One of the strongest fuchsia-reds, flushed purple-magenta with age. Highly perfumed and free-flowering, especially when young, beginning early in the season and recurrent. A short but vigorous shrub, ideal for small gardens. Best if hard-pruned.

'Rose de Rescht'

'Rose du Roi'
Lelieur, France, 1815   90 × 90cm (3 × 3ft)

A magnificent member of the family and a direct offspring of the
'Portland Rose'. It became one of the parents of the first Hybrid
Perpetuals. Called 'Rose Lelieur' by its breeder, and later dedicated to the king by Souchet, of the gardens of Louis XVIII at St
Cloud. The large, loosely double blooms are crimson, flushed
and mottled with purple, and strongly scented. A short but
spreading bush with small, dark green leaves.

'Rose du Roi à Fleurs Pourprés'
Lelieur, France, 1815   75 × 75cm (2½ × 2½ft)

This rose is thought to be a sport from 'Rose du Roi'. In shape it
is very similar, but the flowers have slightly fewer petals and are
rich purple. Another sport, 'Rose du Roi Panache', has pale
flesh-coloured, faintly striped crimson flowers, but is now
rarely seen; it was well known in North America. Graham Stuart
Thomas writes that a bush of this variety was given to him by
Mr George Salmon of Dundrum, who tells that his mother
obtained stock of it from an old garden in
Northern Ireland in 1893.

'Yolande d'Aragon'
Vibert, France, 1843   1.5 × 0.9m (5 × 3ft)

A sumptuous rose which is often included amongst the Hybrid
Perpetuals. Superb, fully double, globular blooms of very
bright, rich pink, and highly scented. Healthy, vigorous, upright
shrub with bright green leaves.

BOURBON ROSES

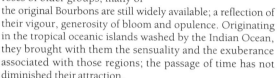

A little history

The Bourbons were the undisputed queens of the garden in the 19th century, dethroned only at the turn of the century by the Hybrid Perpetuals; unlike many of the roses of older groups, many of

Rosa × bourboniana

the original Bourbons are still widely available; a reflection of their vigour, generosity of bloom and opulence. Originating in the tropical oceanic islands washed by the Indian Ocean, they brought with them the sensuality and the exuberance associated with those regions; the passage of time has not diminished their attraction.

The first Bourbons came from the Île de Bourbon, now Réunion, east of Madagascar, where it was the custom to grow rose hedges as field boundaries. Before the opening of the Suez canal, Réunion was an important port of call for French vessels trading between the Far East and Europe, and both *R. chinensis* and the European Autumn Damask were grown there. The initial cross was spontaneous, and the seedlings then known as Rose Édouard were observed by Monsieur Bréon, a French botanist, and Director of the Botanic Gardens there. M. Bréon collected their seeds, and in 1817 sent them to various French gardeners including M. Jacques, head gardener to the Duke of Orléans, in Paris. It is almost certain that Rose Édouard was also grown in the Botanical Gardens of Calcutta at the same time, but the seeds that arrived in France are the ones that are of greater importance in the history of the rose. Unlike the refractory Portlands, they were very fertile, and easy to breed from.

In fact, the first French Bourbon, *Rosa × bourboniana* or Bourbon Rose – no longer in existence – was created by M. Jacques very soon after the arrival of the first seed. It was painted by Redouté in 1824. It had large, semi-double blooms of an intense bright pink, was wonderfully scented with almost evergreen leaves, and had excellent repeat flowering in the autumn. Horticulturists set to work immediately – especially in France, which is why Bourbons remain typically French roses – and work continued unabated until around

1870; the Bourbons multiplied and were greeted with enormous enthusiasm by the fervent public of the time. They were loved for their lengthy, generous flowering (often repeat-flowering), for their vigour, their fragrance, and their sensuality. Their historical contribution is also vital: when crossed with the Portland-China 'Rose du Roi' they gave rise to the *Hybrides remontants* – the Hybrid Perpetuals, – and when crossed with the tea-scented Chinas 'Hume's Blush' and 'Park's Yellow', they gave rise to a new class of Tea roses.

Characteristics

Bourbons are generally large shrubs of great vigour (commonly making 1.8m (6ft) in height and spread) with robust, arching, thorny stems clothed in smooth and substantial foliage. Many can be trained to climb, given the support of pillars, walls and tripods, and the most vigorous can be pegged down to the horizontal to induce flowering all along the length of the stem. Several will climb to a height of 4–5m (12–15ft). These include: 'Blairi No.2', 'Zéphirine Drouhin', and 'Climbing Souvenir de la Malmaison'. The flowers are usually rounded, with gracefully overlapping petals: those of the early hybrids are, for the most part, semi-double, later arrivals have double, goblet-shaped blooms. Only a few are globular. Some maintain Damask characteristics ('Bourbon Queen' and 'Souvenir de la Malmaison') while others indicate their Chinese ancestry (' La Reine Victoria'). The diversity of colour ranges through all shades of reds and pinks, from lighter tones to crimsons and purples; some are ranked among the most beautiful of variegated roses, for example 'Honorine de Brabant'. In cool maritime climates such as that in Britain, they begin blooming in early summer, earlier in warm temperate regions; some Bourbons, such as 'Louise Odier' and 'Zéphirine Drouhin' will repeat reliably until autumn, and sometimes a little later in the year.

Cultivation

Grow in deep, fertile, and moisture-retentive soil, approximately neutral, and enriched with well-rotted organic matter. A mulch of the same is beneficial. Feed with a general rose fertiliser in early spring, and again after the first flush of bloom. In late winter/early spring, cut back stems by about one third, and shorten the longest laterals (sideshoots). Remove dead, weak and very old growth at the same time. These are long-lived shrubs, and once established, the regular removal of very old growth is necessary to allow light and air to young growth which will sprout from the base. Congested plants encourage the presence of disease.

'Bourbon Queen'
('Queen of Bourbons',
'Reine de l'Île Bourbon')

'Adam Messerich'

P. Lambert, Germany, 1920   1.5 × 1.2m (5 × 4ft)

One of the last Bourbons, not really typical, but deserving of
more attention. Bears clusters of semi-double, cupped blooms,
bright rose paling to soft pink in the sun. Strong scent, reminiscent of crushed raspberries. Begins flowering in early summer,
with several flushes until autumn. An upright, vigorous, well-
branched shrub with glossy leaves. Although usually classified
as a Bourbon rose, it is sometimes just listed as a twentieth-
century shrub rose. This is because of its mixed parentage and
late introduction.

ORIGIN: 'Frau Oberhofgartner Singer' × ('Louise Odier' seedling
× 'Louis Philippe')

'Blairi No.1', and 'Blairi No. 2'

Blair, Great Britain, 1845   4 × 1.8m (12 × 6ft) or more

Two climbers, not easily placed, and variously described as
Bourbon, China Hybrids or Teas. 'Blairi No.1' ('Park's Yellow'
tea-scented China × an unnamed hardy rose) has been quite difficult to obtain. It bears, plump, flat, and rather blowsy blooms
of soft blush-pink, fragrant but with a reputation for being shy-
flowering. 'Blairi No.2', a cross between a China rose and
'Tuscany', (in some works described as an offspring of 'Park's
Yellow') is more reliably and freely blooming, once in summer,
with a lesser flush in autumn. Flowers are flat and full, deep
pink, paler at edges, with a delightful spicy perfume. Hardy and
needing very little pruning. Of these two climbers, 'Blairi No. 2'
is more readily available from nurseries, although 'Blairi No.1' is
still sold by specialist suppliers.

'Boule de Neige'

Lacharme, France, 1867   1.2 × 0.9m (4 × 3ft)

A favourite Bourbon bearing small clusters of rounded, crimson buds that open to silky, fully double, camellia-like blooms of a lovely ivory-white, flushed red at the margins. Highly fragrant, in bloom from mid-summer to autumn. An elegant shrub with upright, slender, almost thornless stems, and glossy, dark green and somewhat leathery leaves.

ORIGIN: 'Blanche Lafitte' × 'Sappho'

'Bourbon Queen'
('Queen of Bourbons',
'Reine de l'Île Bourbon')

Mauget, France, 1834   1.8 × 1.5m (6 × 5ft)

A free-flowering Bourbon over a long season in summer, with a few sporadic flowers into autumn. Large, semi-double, cup-shaped flowers, magenta-pink, darker in the centre and paler at the edge, highly scented, followed by large hips. A vigorous shrub with many stout stems and luxuriant light green, blue-tinted foliage. Useful as a pillar rose; will climb to 2m (6ft) with support from a rustic pole or tripod.

'Commandant Beaurepaire'
('Panaché d'Angers')

Moreau-Robert, France, 1874   1.5 × 1.5m (5 × 5ft)

An extraordinary rose with large, double, very fragrant blooms of striking colour; shades of cerise, crimson, and vermilion, marbled and striped with bluish pink and purple. Blooms strongly in summer, rarely again in autumn. A vigorous shrub, dense and thorny, with light green foliage. Indeed, because it creates a dense array of shoots, it is essential that it is pruned each year to prevent it from becoming a tangled mass of unsightly and flowerless stems.

'Coupe d'Hébé'

M. Laffay, France, 1840   2 × 1.5m (6 × 5ft)

Medium-sized, double, cupped blooms of bright pink with a paler reverse, richly perfumed. Petals have a waxy texture. The main flush of bloom is in summer, with occasional flushes to autumn. A lax shrub with slender stems which bend to the ground when in bloom. Susceptible to mildew.

ORIGIN: Bourbon × *Rosa chinensis* hybrid

'Great Western'

Laffay, France, 1838   1.5 × 1.2m (5 × 4ft)

An outstanding Bourbon with large, globular, quartered blooms, purple-magenta with darker shadings in the petal folds, exposing a few golden stamens when fully open. Intensely scented. A prickly shrub, producing a fine crop of red hips in autumn.

'Great Western'

'Honorine de Brabant'   🌸 🖼

1.8 × 1.5m (6 × 5ft)

One of the loveliest of striped roses, with large, cupped, quartered flowers, delicately striped lilac, pink and purple, with a
sweet, raspberry fragrance. A long and continuous flowering
season from early summer to autumn. Dense, vigorous, shrub
with few thorns, and ample, light green foliage. Can also be
grown as a small climber.

'Kathleen Harrop'   🌸 🖼

A. Dickson, Great Britain, 1919   3 × 1.8m (10 × 6ft)

A fairly recent sport of 'Zéphirine Drouhin'; a moderately vigorous climber, completely thornless, and in bloom continuously
from early summer to early winter. Blooms are semi-double, of a
delicate shell pink with a darker reverse; sweetly scented.

'Kronprinzessin Viktoria'   🌸 🖼

Spath 1887   1.5 × 1.5m (5 × 5ft)

This is a sport from the famous 'Souvenir de la Malmaison'. The
only difference is that the blooms are milk white, tinted yellow.

'La Reine Victoria'   🌸 🍶

J. Schwartz, France, 1872   1.5 × 0.9m (5 × 3ft)

A classic Bourbon, opulent and fully double, the silky petals
overlapping to form a deep, rounded cup of silvery rose-pink.
Deliciously scented, perpetual, and very free-flowering. An
upright shrub with slender stems, soft bright green leaves, and
red thorns on young shoots. Requires a rich soil and protection
against the pernicious disease, black spot.

'La Reine Victoria'

'Louise Odier' ('Mme de Stella') 🌸 🖼 🌱

M. Margottin, France, 1851   1.5 × 0.9m (5 × 3ft)

If the outstanding trinity 'Louise Odier', 'La Reine Victoria', and
'Mme Pierre Oger' were the only remaining Bourbons, we would
be duly grateful. They make a glorious group planting. 'Louise
Odier' is a superb rose with the classic old rose flower shape, a
long period of continuous flowering, and a delightful scent.
Very double, cupped blooms, warm pink, flushed lilac, in large
clusters which bend the stems to the ground. Dense, vigorous
shrub with plentiful light green leaves. A valuable, reliable rose
which seldom disappoints. Additionally, the blooms are strongly scented; ideal for planting in a fragrant garden formed of
mixed shrubs or just roses.

'Louise Odier'
('Mme de Stella')

'Mme Isaac Pereire'

Garçon, France, 1881 2 × 1.5m (6 × 5ft) or more

Undoubtedly an outstanding rose with many good qualities,
strong and healthy and with very large, showy blooms, but with
a tendency to coarseness. The flowers are neatly quartered on
opening, later more loosely cup-shaped with outer petals reflexing; magenta pink. A very rich perfume that Graham Stuart
Thomas describes as one of the strongest. The first blooms may
suffer malformation because blooms need warm weather to
mature; good blooms are produced in autumn, with more
carmine tones. A tall shrub with lush, dark green leaves, well-
suited to informal plantings. It is also suitable for planting as a
small climber.

'Mme Isaac Pereire'

'Mme Lauriol de Barny'

Trouillard, France, 1868 1.8 × 1.2m (6 × 4ft)

An agreeable fruity fragrance distinguishes this lovely rose with
large, double, flat and quartered, silvery pink blooms. Summer
flowering, and repeating in autumn. A large, vigorous, and
healthy shrub, the long stems arching under the weight of flowers; they can be pegged down to produce bloom along the
length of the stem.

'Mme Pierre Oger'

Introduced by C. Verdier in 1878 1.8 × 1.2m (6 × 5ft)

A chance discovery by M. Oger, and a worthy sport of 'La Reine
Victoria', the rose from which it stems. The blooms are paler, a
soft mother-of-pearl pink, with ivory highlights, and a crimson
flush in warm weather. The delicate and translucent texture of
the petals bears comparison with water-lilies. Continuous
flowering, from early summer to autumn.

'Reine Victoria'
Schwartz 1872   1.8 × 90cm (6 × 3ft)

A superb shrub rose, with cupped, shell-like, scented, warm
rose-pink flowers. The growth is arching and lax and creates a
rounded shrub.

'Souvenir de la Malmaison'

'Souvenir de la Malmaison'
Jean Béuze, France, 1843   1.2 × 1.2m (4 × 4ft) or more

In memory of Empress Joséphine and her precious garden. One
of the loveliest and most refined, and unlikely ever to fall into
oblivion. The large, cupped flowers, quartered and flat, are
flesh-pink, shaded with grey, and assume creamy tones with
age. Sweetly scented with a hint of spice. Distinguished by a
very long season of bloom: repeating, in a warm climate from
spring to early winter, beautiful in the later months of the year.
Tends to ball in wet weather. The climbing form (Bennett 1893)
may reach 4m (12ft) or more in height. It bears large, blush-
pink, globular flowers.
ORIGIN: 'Mme Desprez' × a Tea Rose

'Souvenir de St Anne's'
                                        1.8 × 1.8m (6 × 6ft)

A foundling, discovered in the garden of Lady Ardilaun, at St
Anne's, near Dublin, and introduced by Graham Stuart Thomas
in 1950. Bears very beautiful, almost single, blush-pink blooms
with graceful, rounded petals, of delicate texture, flushed with
warmer colour at the centre, which holds a cluster of golden
stamens. A robust shrub, flowering freely in summer, and
recurrent in autumn.
ORIGIN: sport of 'Souvenir de la Malmaison'

'Variegata di Bologna'

Introduced by Bonfiglioli, Italy, 1909   2 × 1.2m (6 × 4ft)

Massimiliano Lodi created this rose with globular, double blooms, irregularly streaked with crimson on an ivory-white ground. Strongly scented, blooming in profusion in mid-summer, with a lesser flush in autumn. Lax shrub with few thorns, and rather coarse leaves.

'Zéphirine Drouhin'

Bizot, France, 1868   3 × 1.8m (10 × 6ft) or more

A vigorous shrub reaching over 4m (12ft) as a climber. Much valued for prolific and continuous blooming from summer into autumn, and for being almost totally free of thorns, which more than compensates for the shape of the flowers. Rather loose double, sweetly fragrant, deep cerise-pink, with soft, light green leaves. Prone to mildew and black spot. Suitable for north walls, and hedging. 'Kathleen Harrop', a climbing sport of 'Zéphirine Drouhin', has soft pink, very fragrant blooms. Many rosarians find it a more pleasing colour but it has never equalled 'Zéphirine Drouhin' in popularity. Additionally, it is not quite so vigorous, but in small gardens this is an advantage.

'Zéphirine Drouhin'

NOISETTE ROSES

A little history

Rosa de Phillipe Noisette

The origin of the Noisettes is better documented and less confused than that of other groups. They are descendants of *Rosa moschata,* a semi-climbing rose with loose clusters of small, musk-scented blooms, and a China rose. Noisettes owe two interesting qualities to *R. moschata:* their sweet fragrance and late flowering which, combined with the repeat-flowering of the China rose, resulted in a long season of bloom. The Noisette story begins in South Carolina with the arrival of 'Parson's Pink China'. Easily grown, fertile, hence good for hybridisation, it was crossed with *R. moschata* in 1802 by John Champneys, a wealthy Charleston plantation owner. The result was a splendid climber with clusters of pink flowers, 'Champney's Pink Cluster'. Seeds from this plant were grown on in the Charleston nursery of Phillipe Noisette, who sent a selection of the seedlings to his brother Louis in Paris. Among these was 'Blush Noisette', considered the most important of the group, and illustrated by Redouté in 1821. A few years later, crosses of 'Blush Noisette' with 'Park's Yellow' tea-scented China gave rise to the climbing, yellow-flowered Noisettes, beautifully coloured but more delicate. A small group of delightful plants with lemon, green and gold, primrose, sulphur and golden yellow flowers were produced, and some of them – 'Maréchal Niel', 'Desprez à Fleurs Jaunes', 'Céline Forestier' – are still to be seen in modern gardens.

Characteristics and cultivation

Almost all Noisettes are climbing roses of moderate vigour with long, slender stems, few thorns, glossy leaves, and clusters of small, usually double, rosette-form flowers resembling those of *R. moschata*. They are loved primarily for their grace and refinement, none of them are loud or showy in bloom, and they are often regarded as being somewhat specialist in their appeal. Nevertheless, those that have grown them prize them for the radiance of their bloom, and for the delicate, slightly spicy fragrance.

The later varieties, and those with yellow flowers have a reputation for tenderness, although most are far more cold tolerant than is commonly believed, and will survive occasional lows to −15°C (5°F). All are best planted against a warm, sunny, and sheltered south or south-west wall, where wood will ripen fully. Ripe wood is hardier, and will produce more flowers. Grow in moderately fertile, moisture-retentive but well-drained soil.

Noisettes should be trained so as to form a permanent framework of branches and should be pruned in late winter-early spring by removing weak growth, and cutting back laterals (sideshoots) to about 7.5cm (3in), so that each has two or three buds. Established plants need to have the oldest growth removed periodically, cutting out at the base to encourage replacement growth.

'Aimée Vibert'

'Aimée Vibert'

J. P. Vibert, France, 1828   4 × 3m (12 × 10ft)

Ellen Willmott, Gertrude Jekyll and Graham Stuart Thomas considered this rose the best white-flowered climber ever raised, a rose that at its appearance 'brought the British to their knees'. The double, pure white, fragrant blooms are carried in small clusters at the top of slender stems: blooming in mid-summer, and repeating in autumn in mild weather. A vigorous, healthy climber, with few thorns, and the fine, glossy dark green leaves of *Rosa sempervirens*. This rose can also be grown as a shrub in a border.

ORIGIN: 'Champney's Pink Cluster' × a *Rosa sempervirens* hybrid

'Alister Stella Gray'
('Golden Rambler')
A. S. Gray, introduced by G. Paul & Son in 1894   3 × 3m (10 × 10ft)

Slender, pointed, yolk-yellow buds, tightly packed, open to
double, rosette-form, quartered blooms, buff-yellow, paler at
edges, and creamy white with age. Very pleasing fragrance with
notes of moss and tea. The first flush of small blooms in mid-
summer is followed by a second with larger trusses produced on
new shoots. To 5m (15ft) on a wall. Dark green leaves and a few
scattered thorns.

'Blush Noisette'
L. Noisette, France, 1817   2.5 × 2m (8 × 6ft)

The best among the seedlings grown in Paris by Louis Noisette,
marketed in 1825 under the name of 'Blush Noisette', this very
pretty rose is seldom without a flower from mid-summer to
autumn. Blooms are medium-sized, semi-double, blush-pink,
flushed lilac, with a spicy clove scent, opening to reveal a golden
tuft of stamens. Fairly vigorous shrub, sometimes disinclined to
climb, but always proves a good pillar rose. Thorns are few and
leaves dark green.

'Céline Forestier'
Trouillard, France, 1842   2 × 1.2m (6 × 4ft)

Admirable for its large, elegant, double, flat and quartered
blooms of soft primrose yellow, sometimes tinged with pink
and with a button eye. Flowers profusely and continuously, but
needs a warm sheltered position to do well. Agreeable, spicy
scent, and abundant, light green leaves. May reach 5m (15ft)
against a wall in good conditions. Unfortunately, it is not an
easy rose to grow, but certainly one of the most beautiful.

'Cloth of Gold'
('Chromatella')
Coquereau, France, 1843   4 × 3.5m (12 × 11ft)

Widely grown in the last century and still found in cultivation.
Fully double blooms of soft sulphur yellow with a darker centre,
carried all along the stout shoots: scented and recurrent but
rather tender. Copious light green foliage. Needs a sheltered
position, in full sun, or makes a superb specimen when planted
in a cold glasshouse.

'Crépuscule'
Dubreuil, France, 1904   3.5 × 1.5m (11 × 5ft)

One of the latest Noisettes, with double, shapely blooms,
orange-apricot fading to cream. Needs a protected, very sunny
position. Do not plant it against a cold wall. Free-flowering and
recurrent, with good foliage and few thorns.

'Desprez à Fleurs Jaunes' ('Jaune Desprez')

Desprez, France, 1830   6 × 3m (20 × 10ft)

One of the early Noisettes, and justifiably famous. The exceptional, silk-textured blooms, flat, double, and very neatly
quartered on opening, are rich yellow with peach and apricot
tints, and carried singly or in small clusters from mid-summer
into autumn. They have a fruity scent curiously reminiscent of
banana. Vigorous, smooth-stemmed, but must be given a very
large, warm wall.

ORIGIN: 'Blush Noisette' × 'Park's Yellow' tea-scented China

'Gloire de Dijon'

Jacatot 1853   5 × 4m (15 × 12ft)

A superb rose and widely grown in cottage gardens, where it
was often known as the 'Old Glory Rose'. Its large, globular,
buff-yellow flowers, sometimes tinted pink and gold, appear
through much of summer. The flowers drench gardens in a rich
and somewhat heady fragrance.

'Mme Alfred Carrière'

J. Schwartz, France, 1879   6 × 3m (20 × 10ft)

Of unknown parentage and sometimes included amongst the
Bourbons or Teas, but a glorious specimen whatever its classification. Bears splendid, cup-shaped blooms, white sometimes
tinged blush-pink, intensely scented. Reliable, healthy, and
hardy, growing vigorously, and with long and prolific blooming. Beautiful old specimens can be admired in the famous
garden at Sissinghurst, Kent.

'Maréchal Niel'
Pradel, France, 1864 4.5 × 2.5m (12 × 8ft)

A very famous Tea-Noisette, worthy of note, even by Proust.
Admired for its colour, coppery gold with green tints, for its
gracefully drooping and languid blooms, and its unrivalled tea
fragrance, these virtues enhanced by its dark, purple-flushed
leaves. It is not very hardy, and needs a warm, very sheltered
position outside, thriving in a Mediterranean-type climate,
where it will tolerate part-shade. In cool, maritime climates,
such as that in Britain, it gives of its best under glass.
ORIGIN: probably a seedling of 'Cloth of Gold'

'Maréchal Niel'

'Rêve d'Or'
Veuve Ducher, France, 1869 3.5 × 2.5m (10 × 8ft)

Much used for crossbreeding, especially by Reverend
Pemberton, because of its hardier disposition. The splendid
group of *R. moschata* hybrids was one of the most interesting
results of his work. Bears well-shaped, fully double blooms,
buff-yellow turning butter yellow, sometimes with a touch of
pink. Scented, and repeats well, from early summer. Vigorous,
with glossy leaves, bronze-tinted when young. Hardy, but best
against a warm, sheltered wall.

BOURSAULT
ROSES

A small group of French origin which has been almost completely forgotten, but which really deserves some attention, if only for 'Mme Sancy de Parabère'.

They bear the name of Monsieur Boursault, who gardened in Paris around 1800, and who possessed an extensive rose collection; he was probably the first to breed and grow them. There is little agreement about their provenance. Once thought to be derived from crosses between *R. chinensis* and *R. pendulina,* although their genetic complement is more suggestive of *R. chinensis* with *R. majalis* or *R. blanda.*

They enjoyed a brief period of fame, from 1822 – the year of their official recognition – and constituted a scant group of varieties; worthy of note are 'Amadis' (Crimson Boursault) created by Laffay in 1829, and 'Calypso' (Blush Boursault) in 1848. Their lack of scent, a tendency to produce poorly formed blooms, and above all their recalcitrance in hybridisation, condemned them. Those that survive may prove difficult to obtain.

The Boursaults are large shrubs or semi-climbers with much the same needs in cultivation as the Bourbons. Earlier, in North America, the Boursault 'Amadis' was popular as a understock (rootstock); its roots have a suckering habit, are persistent and last for many years.

'Mme Sancy de Parabère' 🚫 ❀

Bonnet, France, 1874   4.5 × 3m (13 × 10ft)

A beautiful and interesting climber but with two drawbacks: perfume is missing and flowers are produced only in early or mid-summer. The blooms are up to 12cm (5in) across, soft pink, and loosely double with an unusual formation: they bear an inner rosette of short, curled petals, surrounded by an outer rank of larger ones. Very hardy, with thornless shoots, and dark green, finely toothed leaves.

TEA ROSES

A little history

The Tea roses, so-named for their delicate, spicy scent that is suggestive of fresh leaves of China tea, are somewhat tender shrubs of oriental grace that trace their origins to *Rosa × odorata*, a hybrid of

Rosa × odorata

R. gigantea and *R. chinensis*. Long cultivated and with many varieties in China, the West has seen but few of these, the most famous being 'Hume's Blush' tea-scented China and 'Park's Yellow' tea-scented China (see China roses). The official title of first European Tea rose was assigned to the yellow-flowered 'Safrano', created in 1839.

Following the introduction of 'Safrano', the work of hybridisation became more systematic, better documented and more precise. Professional breeders were inspired to perform crosses and back-crosses to yield ever more complex hybrids, and – when the outcome was favourable – to present their new progeny to an expectant public. The Tea roses grown in the 19th century had an extraordinarily complicated and broadly based genetic complement with an admixture of chromosomes derived, above all, from crosses between Chinas, Bourbons and Noisettes. Thus it is that in some the characteristics of one parent group prevails, whilst in others one sees clearly the attributes of another, more distant progenitor, a Damask, for example, or *Rosa gigantea*. This leads to confusion, and it is common that varieties cannot, with confidence, definitely be assigned to one group. We see in the literature that famous roses like 'Gloire de Dijon' or 'Mme Alfred Carrière' have variously been assigned to the Noisettes, Bourbons or Teas. Tea roses do not always appear to be Tea roses, and their direct descendants, the Hybrid Teas, derived from crossings with Hybrid Perpetuals, only become a category in their own right in the 20th century.

With few exceptions, Tea roses are perhaps the least remembered of 19th century roses. The primary reason for this is their delicate nature, their need for sun, warmth and protection. Loved and grown mainly in the gardens of aristocratic mansions on the Mediterranean coast, and in Victorian conservatories, they were, unfortunately, destined to fade away with the gradual disappearance of their owners, succumbing to the blows dealt by their more robust and arrogant rivals, the Hybrid Perpetuals, finally to be deposed by the now commonplace, hybrid descendants which still bear part of their name and rich ancestry.

Characteristics and cultivation

The Tea roses are remontant climbers or slender shrubs with glossy, usually pale green leaves, and few thorns. They have exceptionally elegant buds, long, slender and pointed, on fragile stems that often droop under the weight of the flower. Double or semi-double, sometimes quartered on opening, the long, elegant petals are often higher in the centre, heralding the form of the Hybrid Teas, and prized for exhibition. Flowering begins early in summer and is usually continuous; some are repeat-flowering. Tea roses are characterised by their subdued pastel shades, pale yellows, buffs and pinks of subtle and translucent beauty, often almost transparent, so as to move William Robinson to describe them as the colours of the clouds. This famous Irish gardener and writer wrote, among many other works, *The English Flower Garden*. It was first published in 1883 and ran to more than fifteen editions.

Most are best suited to Mediterranean-type climates, such as those of California and parts of Australia, and even the hardiest need a warm, sunny site sheltered from frosts in cooler regions.

The shrubs are suitable for growing in tubs and large pots; the climbers, which are also usually the most rewarding, are ideal against warm, sheltered walls. The more formal are perfect for glasshouses and conservatories. The former require minimal pruning, the latter none whatsoever. Otherwise grow as for Noisettes. They may be difficult to find and acquire, even from the specialist growers. However there are several nurseries which still grow them and national rose societies are often able to offer advice about suppliers. Additionally, there are specialist booklets which are updated every year and list the names of nurseries which offer specific varieties.

'Adam'

Adam, 1833   2.2 × 1.5m (7 × 5ft)

One of the first of the British Tea roses. Blooms are large, very double and quartered when fully open, amber and apricot, flushed pink at the petal base, recurrent and scented. Vigorous shrub with ample, dark foliage which can be grown as a climber on a wall. Tends to ball in wet weather. This early Tea rose – said to be the first typical Pink Tea Rose – was raised by a florist named Adam in Reims in 1833, and is still available from specialist rose nurseries.

'Archiduc Joseph'

'Anna Olivier'
Ducher, France, 1872   90 × 90cm (3 × 3ft)

Well-shaped, double, high-centred blooms are pink with
salmon shadings. Scented. A long flowering season, in summer.
Vigorous, with stout shoots and ample foliage that give this
shrub an added quality.

'Archiduc Joseph'
Gilbert Nabonnand, France, 1872   1.5 × 0.9m (5 × 3ft)

A magnificent rose with double blooms of unusual colouring: a
mixture of pink, purple and orange with flashes of gold at the
centre. Long and generous flowering. Hardier than most, with
few thorns and abundant, glossy dark green leaves. Can be
grown as a small climber, although it is always far prettier when
grown as a bush.
ORIGIN: 'Mme Lombard seedling'

'Baronne Henriette de Snoy'
A. Bernaix, France, 1897   1.2 × 0.9m (4 × 3ft)

High-centred, elegant buds open to well-formed, agreeably
scented, flesh pink blooms with a carmine-pink reverse. Stems
of an angular growth and ample foliage.
ORIGIN: 'Gloire de Dijon' × 'Mme Lombard'

'Belle Lyonnaise'
Levet, France, 1870   3 × 1.8m (10 × 6ft)

Large, fragrant, fully double, flat and quartered blooms are soft
creamy yellow fading to cream at margins. Shrub or small
climber, very free-flowering, ideal for sheltered, sunny sites, or
the cold greenhouse.

'Clementina Carbonieri'   🌺 ⛁ 🏵 ☀
Bonfiglioli, Italy, 1913   90 × 60cm (3 × 2ft)

The double, flat and quartered blooms are an interesting combination of pink, salmon, and orange on a mustard-yellow
ground, and despite the impression of vulgarity that this
description conjures, this is actually a very lovely rose. Scented
and very free-flowering, forming a dense, fairly prickly bush,
with an abundance of dark leaves.

'Devoniensis, Climbing'   🌺 ⛁ 🏵 ☀
('Magnolia Rose')
Pavitt, Curtis, Great Britain, 1858   3.5 × 2m (11 × 6ft)

An exquisitely refined, climbing Tea with large, creamy white
blooms, sometimes flushed pink; very double, flat and quartered, and intensely fragrant. A recurrent climber with light
green leaves and few thorns. It needs a warm protected position,
but well worth finding space in the cold glasshouse where its
perfection can best be appreciated.
ORIGIN: Climbing sport of 'Devoniensis', raised by Foster,
1838

'Dr Grill'   🌺 ⛁ 🏵 ☀
Bonnaire, France, 1886   90 × 60cm (3 × 2ft)

A rose with elegant, high-centred buds opening to flat, fully
double, sometimes quartered blooms, coppery pink and well
scented. Recurrent and free-flowering. A climber with few
thorns and scant foliage.
ORIGIN: 'Ophirie' × 'Souvenir de Victor Hugo'

'Duchesse de Brabant'   🌺 ⛁ 🏵
Bernède, France, 1857   90 × 90cm (3 × 3ft)

Once popular and much loved, but unfortunately no longer easily available. Bears cupped, fully double flowers, soft to deep
pink, very fragrant and carried freely from early summer to late
autumn. A very hardy plant, of bushy, open and spreading
habit, with abundant foliage. This superb variety is said to have
been the favourite rose of President Theodore Roosevelt and
often worn in the lapel of his coat.

'Général Gallieni'   🌺 ⛁ 🏵 ☀
Gilbert Nabonnand, France, 1899   1.2 × 0.9m (4 × 3ft)

Very famous and much appreciated in its hey-day. Bears irregularly cup-shaped blooms whose colour changes with age and
season, from buff-yellow to copper, chestnut-red and dark red.
Robust, with smooth, green stems and plentiful foliage. Its popularity has waned during the last fifty years, although it is still
sold by specialist nurseries.
ORIGIN: 'Souvenir de Thérèse Levet' × 'Reine Emma des Pays-Bas'

'Gloire de Dijon'

'Général Schablikine'

Gilbert Nabonnand, France, 1878   90 × 60cm (3 × 2 ft)

Of unknown parentage, but shows an affinity with *Rosa chinensis* in its purplish young shoots, and with *R. × odorata* in its slender flower stems. Bears flat, double, cherry-red blooms with copper-bronze highlights, and rich fragrance. A profuse first flowering is followed by two lesser flushes. Compact and attractive bush with dense foliage.

'Gloire de Dijon'

Jacotot, France, 1853   5 × 4m (15 × 12ft)

One of the best known of old Teas, and a Victorian favourite. Often classed with the Noisettes. First named the Old Glory Rose, for its splendid colour, buff-yellow, tinged with apricot, and pinker in warm conditions, fading to cream. The very large blooms are full, flat and irregularly quartered, with deliciously fruity scent. It flowers profusely at the beginning of summer and again in autumn. Indeed, it is seldom out of flower from mid-summer onwards. Hardy, but prone to black spot if stressed; does well on north walls.

ORIGIN: a Yellow tea-scented China × 'Souvenir de la Malmaison'

'Lady Hillingdon'

Lowe and Shawyer, Great Britain, 1910   90 × 60cm (3 × 2ft)

A fairly recent variety with pointed buds opening to large, sweetly scented, semi-double, apricot-yellow flowers, beautifully offset against coppery stems. Few thorns, and dark purplish green leaves. 'Climbing Lady Hillingdon', introduced by Hicks in 1917; less tender than generally thought, may reach 5m (15ft) or more.

ORIGIN: 'Papa Gontier' × 'Mme Hoste'

'Maman Cochet'
S. Cochet, 1893   90 × 60cm (3 × 2ft)

Large, high-centred, globular and rather blowsy when fully
open, the flowers are soft pink with darker shading, flushed
lemon at the petal base. Much grown for exhibition in the 19th
century, but now superseded, especially in the USA, by its sport
'White Maman Cochet'. A vigorous bush, almost thornless, with
dark, leathery leaves.
ORIGIN: 'Marie von Houtte' × 'Mme Lombard'

'Mme de Tartas'
Bernède, France, 1859   90 × 90cm (3 × 3ft)

An important rose, much used at the end of the last century for
breeding. Bears large, fully double, cup-shaped blooms, blush-
pink, and fragrant. Vigorous, open shrub with dark, leathery
leaves. Unfortunately, it is very difficult to acquire. One of the
hardier Tea roses.

'Mme Jules Gravereaux'
Soupert & Notting, Luxembourg, 1901   2.5 × 1.5m (8 × 5ft) or more

A sumptuous rose, with beautifully shaped blooms, quartered,
fully double, outer petals reflexing, warm buff-pink, with yellow
tints; deliciously fruity, tea scented. A vigorous shrub or climber
to 4m (12ft) with abundant, glossy, dark green leaves. Hardy
against a warm, south-facing wall.
ORIGIN: 'Rêve d'Or' × 'Viscountess Folkstone'

'Lady Hillingdon'

'Niphetos'

Bougère, France, 1843 1.2 × 0.9m (4 × 3ft)

One of the oldest, a florist's flower, grown under glass in
Victorian times for cutting. Splendid, rosette-form flowers with
pointed petals, pure white, and scented, opening from elegant,
creamy buds. A vigorous shrub which needs a sheltered position, or in cool areas, glasshouse protection, to give its best. The
climbing form (Keynes, Williams and Co. 1889). Often
reaches 3m (10ft) or more high.

'Papa Gontier'
Gilbert Nabonnand, France, 1883 90 × 60cm (3 × 2ft)

Like 'Niphetos', a florist's rose, grown for greenhouse forcing
and cutting. Pointed buds open to bright rose-pink blooms,
carmine on the petal reverse; large, semi-double, only slightly
scented. Well-branched bush, with sparse, but attractive, glossy,
dark green leaves.

'Perle des Jardins'
F. Levet, France, 1874 90 × 60cm (3 × 2ft)

The large, globular, fully double and quartered blooms are sulphur yellow to buff-yellow, and well-scented. Robust, compact
bush with wiry stems, needing a sunny, protected site, or
glasshouse protection for perfect blooms. Quite hardy, but balls
in wet weather.
ORIGIN: a seedling from 'Mme Falcot'

'Rosette Delizy'
P. Nabonnand, France, 1922 90 × 60cm (3 × 2ft)

Not well known but a fine specimen with large, well-formed,
double blooms in a pleasing combination of rose-pink, buff-yellow and apricot, with a darker reverse. It flowers profusely and
has an excellent scent. A well-branched, dense shrub.
ORIGIN: 'Général Gallieni' × 'Comtesse Bardi'

'Safrano'
('Beauregarde')

Beauregard, France, 1839 90 × 60cm (3 × 2ft)

Together with 'Niphetos' one of the first and oldest Teas.
Deserves a place in the garden for its many merits, including
robust good health, and especially for generous, continuous
flowering, from late spring. The elegant, high-pointed buds
open to large, semi-double, apricot blooms, flushed saffron yellow, and fading to cream. Once widely grown as a button-hole
flower. Indeed, for many years this suberb rose was widely in
demand by flower arrangers, especially in North America. It was
grown in greenhouses in the colder part of that continent.
Although introduced more than one hundred and fifty years
ago, it is still available, but only from specialist nurseries.

'Sombreuil'
('Colonial White')

'Sombreuil' ('Colonial White')

Robert, France, 1850 2.5 × 1.5m (8 × 5ft) or more

A climbing Tea with large, double, very flat and tidily quartered blooms, white with a hint of cream at the centre; sweetly scented. A large, lax shrub with ample foliage, or a small climber if grown on a sheltered wall. Quite hardy.

ORIGIN: a seedling from 'Gigantesque' × a Hybrid Perpetual

'Souvenir de Mme Léonie Viennot'

A. Bernaix, France, 1898 3.5 × 2.5m (11 × 8ft)

A climbing Tea, with large, beautifully shaped, fully double blooms of good scent and lovely colouring; a primrose to buff-yellow ground, flushed with orange-copper and pink.

'Souvenir d'un Ami'

Bléot-Defougère, France, 1846 2.5 × 1.5m (8 × 5ft)

A vigorous Tea, with very large, fully double, cupped blooms, soft, salmon-tinted pink on emergence, darkening and developing yellow tints with age. Highly scented. Tall, stout and well-branched shrub or climber.

'William R. Smith' ('Charles Dingee', 'Blush Maman Cochet', 'Président William Smith', 'Jeannette Heller')

Bagg, USA, 1909 90 × 60cm (3 × 2ft)

A rose with a collection of names, a proof of its popularity The large blooms are notable for the graceful arrangement of the silky petals, creamy white, flushed pink, buff and gold at the base. A compact and tidy bush, with stout stems and leathery leaves. Fairly hardy.

ORIGIN: 'Maman Cochet' × 'Mme Hoste'

HYBRID PERPETUAL ROSES

'Rose du Roi'

A little history

In the second half of the
19th century a new breed
of rose comes into the
ascendant, eventually pre-
dominating in popularity over all its
predecessors. Indeed, until the advent of the
Hybrid Teas, no other group of roses received
such an enthusiastic welcome. These roses had all the qualities needed to be successful: a stronger scent than Bourbons,
at times overpowering, a robust constitution, reliably hardy,
superior to the Portlands in compactness and intensity of
colour, and suitable for cutting. Valued for their opulence,
they were produced in hundreds and hundreds of varieties;
the catalogues of the period list over 3000 names, of which
many are still sold and grown in gardens today. And yet the
Hybrides remontant – Hybrid Perpetuals – may be criticised
for one thing: intended for a wider public – the affluent bour-
geoisie – they have more grandeur than charm. They lack the
freshness of an Alba rose, the delicacy of a Damask, the seduction of the Bourbons, the grace of Noisettes. They are roses
which were bred in the period which saw the rise of the great
flower shows on both sides of the English Channel, and there,
in competitive exhibition, they undoubtedly serve their purpose. They were created to be attractive in bud, elegant and
long-stemmed; essential for exhibition. But regal in bud, and
often lovely in flower, they are often singularly lacking in
grace of habit, and frequently fail to enchant.

The ancestor of this group is the Portland × China hybrid
'Rose du Roi', and following some confusion – a rose like 'La
France' was first classified as a Hybrid Perpetual before being
honoured as the original Hybrid Tea – the group acquires
more precise attributes. They are the product of laborious
crosses between Bourbons, Portlands (despite their always
rather limited fertility), China Hybrids (Gallica × China), and
Tea roses, their centre of production being France and their
leading artist Laffay, who, with precise and logical intention,
was performing some 200,000 crosses every year. Laffay takes

the credit for one of the first of the group, 'La Reine' (1842), with silver-pink blooms bearing numerous, serried ranks of petals, and flowering continuously. Between 1837–1843 he puts his name to eighteen more varieties. Several interesting versions were also produced in England, in particular by William Paul. The first Hybrid Perpetuals form a more homogeneous group; those created subsequently reveal substantial differences as to habit, intensity of fragrance and remontancy.

Characteristics

Almost all are extremely vigorous, cold and disease resistant, upright and branching shrubs, although inclined to coarseness. They produce long, vigorous shoots during summer that are well-suited to pegging down to produce bloom along their length. Some are suitable as climbers or 'pillar' roses. The blooms, although often high-pointed in bud, are for the most part rounded, with abundant petals, and a colour range in which reds predominate; deep reds, very dense and devoid of transparency, crimsons, magentas, and purples, with some pinks and whites. Flowering is almost always profuse, continuous or with excellent repeat-flowering in autumn. The scent is intense and intoxicating. Nearly all are invaluable as cut flowers for home decoration.

Cultivation

One of the most interesting ways of growing the more vigorous Hybrid Perpetuals (also suitable for Hybrid Musks) is that developed by Victorian gardeners, known as pegging down. The long shoots of the current season's growth are not pruned back in winter, but are bent over with their tips tied to pegs in the ground. Alternatively they may be tied-in to a low framework, about 60cm (2ft), that surrounds the main trunk. The following season, new laterals form on the pegged shoots, which bear a profusion of bloom so as almost to form a carpet

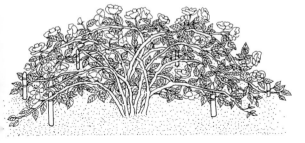

Pegging down

'Baron Girod de l'Ain'

of flower. Since such abundant flower production consumes considerable energy, the Hybrid Perpetuals must have a very fertile soil, enriched with well-rotted organic matter before planting, and top-dressed with bone meal at planting. Mulching with an organic mulch is also recommended. Feed with a balanced rose fertiliser in late winter/early spring, and again in mid-summer after the first flush of bloom. Prune in late winter/early spring; remove weak, dead and badly placed growth, and cut back remaining strong stems by half, to the nearest outward-facing bud. Harder pruning will result in larger but fewer blooms, less severe pruning in small, but more abundant flowers. During all pruning activities, always cut out diseased or pest-infested shoots. Ensure that all prunings are removed and burned to prevent the spread of pests and diseases.

'Ardoisée de Lyon'

Damaizin, France, 1858   1.2 × 0.9m (4 × 3ft)

Little known but deserving attention for its very mannerly, quartered blooms, deep cerise-pink with violet and purple shadings, held on robust and stiff stems; intensely scented. Tidy, compact, and very thorny bush with grey-green leaves.

'Baron Girod de l'Ain'

Reverchon, France, 1897   1.2 × 0.9m (4 × 3ft)

Not widely grown today, but very popular at the turn of the century. Bears large clusters of very double, cupped blooms, bright crimson, with almost fringed, white petal margins, and sweet fragrance. A dense bush but with a tendency to sprawl; has strong, sparse thorns and leathery leaves. It is less richly coloured than 'Roger Lambelin', but is more easily grown and tends to retain its petals better.

ORIGIN: probably a sport of 'Eugène Fürst'

90

'Baroness Rothschild'

Pernet Père, France, 1868   1.2 × 0.9m (4 × 3ft)

An outstanding rose, one of the loveliest of Hybrid Perpetuals.
The very large, flat blooms, carried upright on stiff stems, have
silky petals curving gently to form a wide cup; dark rose-pink,
fading to delicate pink at the margins, and strongly scented.
Flowers profusely and bears ample, grey-green leaves. 'Mabel
Morrison', introduced by Broughton in 1878, is a sport of
'Baroness Rothschild' with pink buds, and white blooms spotted
with pink in warm weather: excellent for cutting.

ORIGIN: a sport of 'Souvenir de la Reine d'Angleterre'

'Baronne Prévost'

Desprez, France, 1842   1.5 × 1.2m (5 × 4ft)

One of the oldest of the group, which disappeared from gardens
and was rediscovered in the United States. A rose of many
virtues, long-lived, and with many-petalled, deep pink blooms,
flat, often quartered, and with a button eye. Scented. Compact,
upright bush, slightly coarse and thorny.

'Charles Lefèbvre'

Lacharme, France, 1861   1.2 × 0.9m (4 × 3ft)

Rich and opulent, with many tightly-packed petals, the widely
cupped blooms are crimson with darker shadings, intensely
fragrant, and held on strong stems. Not always recurrent, but
has exceptionally attractive foliage.

ORIGIN: 'Général Jacqueminot' × 'Victor Verdier'

'Dupuy Jamain'

Jamain, France, 1868   1.2 × 0.9m (4 × 3ft)

A great favourite in Victorian gardens, with double, many-
petalled, cerise-red blooms, held on stiff stems, and richly
perfumed. Upright, healthy bush, almost free of thorns, and
with lush green leaves.

'Empereur du Maroc'

'Ferdinand Pichard'

'Empereur du Maroc'

B. Guinoisseau, introduced by E. Verdier, 1858   1.2 × 0.9m (4 × 3ft)

Appreciated for its compact, deep crimson, velvety blooms held
upright above the leaves, flat, fully double, and with an excellent fragrance. Free-flowering shrub of moderate vigour which
needs protection against black spot and mildew.
ORIGIN: a seedling of 'Géant des Batailles'

'Ferdinand Pichard'

Tanne, 1921   1.5 × 1.2m (5 × 4ft)

A fairly modern member of the group, an interesting rose, one
of the few striped Perpetuals. The large, cupped, almost globular blooms combine crimson and soft pink on a white ground,
with a pleasant, crushed-raspberry fragrance. Healthy, stout
shrub with copious bright green leaves. It is not known if this
was raised from seed or occurred as a sport.

'Frau Karl Druschki' ('Reine des Neiges' etc.)

'Frau Karl Druschki' ('Reine des Neiges', 'Snow Queen', 'White American Beauty')

Peter Lambert, Germany, 1901   1.5 × 0.9m (5 × 3ft)

Perhaps more correctly included amongst the early Hybrid Teas. A lovely rose, still widely grown, but with two drawbacks: blooms have little fragrance, and are quickly spoiled by rain. Elegant, pointed buds open to well-shaped, snow-white flowers with a touch of lemon at the petal base. Recurrent after a long resting period. Robust and vigorous shrub, clothed with abundant, light green, leathery leaves.
ORIGIN: 'Merveille de Lyon' × 'Mme Caroline Testout'

'Général Jacqueminot'

Roussel, France, 1853   1.5 × 1.2m (5 × 4ft)

Or 'Gen Jack', as it is affectionately called, a popular and important rose as one of the parents of many Modern Roses, amongst them 'Crimson Glory'. Of Bourbon descent, it probably originates from 'Gloire des Rosomanes', has a Damask scent and a

'Général Jacqueminot'

Hybrid Tea flower form. Bears a profusion of clear, bright red flowers on long stems in mid-summer, with a second, lesser display in autumn. Reasonably compact shrub, of strong constitution, with bright green leaves.

'Georg Arends' ('Fortune Besson')

W. Hinner, Germany, 1910   1.5 × 1.2m (5 × 4ft)

Although usually included with the Hybrid Perpetuals, bears typical Hybrid Tea blooms, high-centred with reflexing outer petals, pale pink, flushed darker pink at petal margins, and very fragrant. Profuse and continual flowering. A vigorous bush with large, grey-green leaves.
ORIGIN: 'Frau Karl Druschki' × 'La France'

'Gloire de Ducher' ('Germania')

Ducher, France, 1865   1.8 × 1.2m (6 × 4ft)

With its very large, highly scented blooms, crowded with petals of deep pink-crimson, fading to purple, this is amongst the finest of the Hybrid Perpetuals. The second blooming in autumn generally surpasses the first in summer. A tall, but rather lax-growing shrub with long, arching branches and dark green leaves. Susceptible to mildew.

'Gloire Lyonnaise'

Guillot Fils, France, 1885   1.2 × 0.6m (4 × 2ft)

A lovely rose worthy of more attention. The beautiful, cup-shaped blooms are crowded with creamy white petals, flushed lemon at the base; well-scented, and produced freely over a long season. An upright shrub with stiff shoots, few thorns, and healthy, dark, leathery leaves.

ORIGIN: 'Baroness Rothschild' × 'Mme Falcot'

'Hugh Dickson'

H. Dickson, Great Britain, 1905   2.2 × 1m (7 × 3ft)

A fairly recent Hybrid Perpetual with deep crimson, double, high-centred, and very fragrant blooms, carried in great profusion on arching stems clothed with dark leaves. Blooms in summer, and again in autumn. A good pillar rose; excellent for pegging down.

ORIGIN: 'Lord Bacon' × 'Grüss an Teplitz'

'Mrs John Laing'

Henry Bennett, Great Britain, 1887   1.2 × 0.9m (4 × 3ft)

A great favourite of Victorian and Edwardian gardeners, especially for exhibition. A refined plant with clusters of large, cupped, many petalled blooms of soft silvery pink, flushed lilac: good scent, resistant to rain, and repeats well. Free-flowering, upright, sturdy shrub with large, grey-green leaves.

ORIGIN: a seedling of 'François Michelon'

'Paul Neyron'

A. Levet, France, 1869   90 × 60cm (3 × 2ft)

An unforgettable rose, still widely cultivated, and much loved for the exceptionally large blooms of an unfading crimson. Indeed, each flower has an enormous number of petals, about fifty, and often extends to an impressive 15cm (6in) wide. When fully open, each flower exposes a mass of short, muddled petals at its centre. Rich fragrance. Free-flowering and recurrent, a strong, healthy, and upright bush. Leaves are matt dark green. It is ideal as a cut flower for room decoration.

ORIGIN: 'Victor Verdier' × 'Anna de Diesbach'

'Paul Neyron'

'Reine des Violettes' 🌹 🏵
Millet, Malet, France, 1860　　　1.5 × 0.9m (5 × 3ft)

Another very popular rose in its hey-day, with a strong affinity
to the Gallicas, appreciated for the remarkable colour of its
velvety blooms: deep, dusky purple fading to violet. They are
packed with many petals, flat when fully open, quartered, very
well-formed and richly fragrant. An extraordinary rose when in
full bloom, flowering is profuse, and repeats well. A strong,
upright shrub with long, stiff, almost thornless stems, and an
abundance of soft, grey-green leaves. Needs a rich soil and
repays careful cultivation.
ORIGIN: a seedling of 'Pope Pius IX'

'Reine des Violettes'

'Roger Lambelin'

J. Schwartz, France, 1890 1.2 × 0.9m (4 × 3ft)

The unusual shape and the dark velvety colour of blooms recommend this lovely rose. With many irregular, deep crimson petals, fringed and rimmed with white, the flowers are reminiscent of carnations; well-scented but not reliably repeating. Needs fertile soil, careful cultivation and protection against mildew and blackspot.

ORIGIN: a sport of 'Prince Camille de Rohan'

'Sidonie'

'Sidonie'

Vibert, France, 1847 90 × 60cm (3 × 2ft)

Resembling a Portland with open clusters of plump blooms in rich glowing pink, with frilled petal margins. A small, graceful bush, well-suited to small gardens, with large leaves, unfortunately prone to mildew and blackspot.

'Souvenir du Docteur Jamain' ('Souvenir d'Alphonse Levellée')

Lacharme, France, 1865 3 × 2m (10 × 6ft)

Colour and fragrance are the primary merits of this deservedly popular rose. Bears semi-double, cupped blooms of shining, dark ruby-red, but needs protection from the hottest sun if this is not to fade. A sweet, heady fragrance. Flowering in mid-summer, and bears a few flowers in autumn. Tall, spreading and rather lax shrub, with almost thornless stems, and dark green leaves. Graham Stuart Thomas writes that we owe the preservation of this rose to the Hon. V. Sackville-West.

ORIGIN: a seedling of 'Charles Lefèbvre' or 'Général Jacqueminot'

'Ulrich Brunner Fils'

A. Levet, France, 1882   2 × 1m (6 × 3ft)

Used extensively for greenhouse forcing at the turn of the century, this florist's rose is still seen in gardens today. Large, cupped, fleshy blooms are double, but blowsy when fully open, sweetly scented, and held in large clusters on long stems: clear red turning to rosy purple, paler at maturity. Recurrent. Tall, upright, undemanding shrub, with dark green foliage. Tends to ball in wet weather.

ORIGIN: probably an offspring of 'Paul Neyron'

'Vick's Caprice'

Vick, USA, 1891   1.2 × 0.9m (4 × 3ft)

A lovely rose, with large, double, cupped and high-centred blooms, pale pink and lilac, striped and mottled with white and deep pink. Fragrance is sweet and agreeable; flowering season long and repeated. Upright shrub, not very thorny, of moderate vigour. This is an American variety and occurred in the garden of Mr Vick at Rochester, New York.

ORIGIN: a sport of 'Archiduchesse Elisabeth d'Autriche'

'Vick's Caprice'

ENGLISH ROSES

'Gertrude Jekyll'

A little history

Those who have loved Old Roses almost inevitably watch with regret the fading of their glorious, mid-summer abundance. For them, the advent of English Roses in the 1950s has been a just cause for celebration, and echoes the excitement that rosarians of other earlier eras must have felt with the arrival of the Bourbons or Hybrid Perpetuals. They have a sole creator, a 20th-century Laffay, David Austin, who works at Albrighton, Wolverhampton, England, where he has a flourishing nursery and a splendid and extensive collection of very attractive old garden roses.

English roses are simultaneously ancient and modern; the former confirmed by their appearance, the latter undeniable given the year of presentation to the public. With great ingenuity and forethought, Austin has created them by breeding old with new, with one of his primary intentions being the restoration of their dignity as garden shrubs, rather than as graceless, "flower-producing machines" like the Hybrid Teas, often just four bare stems whose only purpose is to bear perfect but haughty blooms. He has created an alliance between old roses and new roses, uniting the best features of both and picking up the thread of their evolution where it was left at the demise of the Bourbons. English roses are, in essence, old garden roses which flower more; they provide us with blooms of exquisite form and every desirable colour, with all the old scents: lemon, raspberry, myrrh and above all the inebriating and ephemeral fragrance of the Gallicas, Albas, Chinas and Damasks. They are elegant and graceful shrubs, well-branched and, for the most part, with an abundance of fine foliage. And they flower continuously or repeat reliably.

David Austin's work began with a cross between two splendid roses, the single-flowered floribunda 'Dainty Maid' and the Gallica 'Belle Isis' with the fortunate outcome being 'Constance Spry'; a large shrub or climber, with deeply cupped, double flowers of luminous, clear pink with a heady scent of myrrh. Although once-flowering, because it lacks the double complement of genes required for remontancy, it undoubtedly illustrates the immense potential of crossing old with new. Austin has continued on these principles, hybridising old roses with selected modern Hybrid Teas and Floribundas carefully chosen for their characteristics: first 'Ma Perkins', 'Dusky Maiden', and 'Chateau de Clos Vougeot' (for deep, velvety reds), 'Mme Caroline Testout', 'Louise Odier', 'Duchesse de Montebello', 'Conrad Ferdinand Meyer' (for their delicious range of satiny pinks) and, among the more recent, 'Iceberg', for its extraordinary repeat-flowering and the beauty of its blooms. And since the gene for repeat-flowering is often accompanied by others determining the form of the flower or the grace of the shrub, Austin has devoted time to a new series of crosses, including some between different English roses themselves, aimed at eliminating the unwanted characteristics of new roses. To this end, he has even gone so far as withdrawing from the market some of his own well-known and magnificent roses, such as 'The Friar' or 'Admired Miranda', because they are not deemed "old" enough.

In this way, following patient and rigorous selection, extraordinary and increasingly sophisticated English roses are presented annually to the public, and find their way into gardens all over the world. Since others, such as Ralph Sievers, of Kiel (Germany), working mainly with Alba roses, have followed the trail laid by Austin, it is certain that for the immediate future we can count on an ever-increasing number of new roses with all the enchanting virtues of their well-known and ancient parents.

'The Friar'

Characteristics

Most English roses have double flowers with some of the loveliest forms that roses have ever possessed. Deep goblets full of fragrance, flat and quartered cups which seem to have been trimmed with scissors and packed with perfect petals, symmetrical rosette forms, roses domed like peonies or gardenias. Many are cluster-flowered, either refinedly so, or with blooms stacked one above the other with almost baroque exuberance. There are few English roses with single or semi-double blooms, but among these 'Dapple Dawn', 'Windrush', 'Redcoat' and 'Wild Flower' are worthy of note.

The range of colours is enormous; an extraordinary variety of pinks, flesh-pink, shell-pink, peach and apricot, lilac-pink fading to grey-pink – but also many reds from magenta to scarlet, and velvety, deep wine reds; yellows from sulphur to gold and orange, and whites of all tones.

Their fragrance, often surpassing even those of the Old Roses in intensity, encompasses a whole gamut of perfumes with fruity and green-tea notes, include a spicy, myrrh-like scent which Austin considers typical of the group.

English roses vary in height and spread from 90–150cm (3–5ft), and are robust, vigorous shrubs of graceful and shapely habit, flowering continuously or repeatedly from early or mid-summer. Some are grown as small climbers.

Cultivation

Being repeat-flowering, English Roses need very fertile soil, enriched with well-rotted organic matter before planting, and top-dressed with bone meal at planting. Mulching with an organic mulch is also recommended. Feed with a balanced rose fertiliser in late winter/early spring, and again in mid-summer after the first flush of bloom. They require no pruning in their first year. In subsequent seasons, prune in late winter/early spring; remove weak, dead, and badly placed growth, and cut back remaining strong stems by one third to one half, to the nearest outward-facing bud. Harder pruning will result in larger but fewer blooms, less severe pruning in small, but more abundant flowers. As plants mature, remove some of the oldest growth to allow new growth to sprout from the base. Dead head as blooms fade, cutting back to the nearest full-sized leaf. Remove suckers as seen. These roses are usually resistant to cold, wet, and disease.

'Wild Flower'

Other than in very small gardens, English Roses are best grown in groups of three. They associate well with Old Roses, and are well-suited to informal, mixed borders, and cottage garden plantings where they mix with other plants.

'Abraham Darby'

David Austin, Great Britain, 1985   1.5 × 1.5m (5 × 5ft)

Exceptionally large, and beautifully formed blooms, deeply cupped and quartered, in tones of peach, apricot and yellow. Abundant and repeated flowering, beginning in early summer. Good fruity fragrance. An excellent, healthy shrub, with arching branches and glossy leaves, reaching 3m (10ft) if grown as a climber. This is one of the Larger English Roses and highly recommended for planting at the back of a border.
ORIGIN: 'Yellow Cushion' × 'Aloha'

'Admired Miranda'

David Austin, 1982   90 × 60cm (3 × 2ft)

If you grow this rose, cherish it, as it is no longer listed in the Austin catalogue. Elegant, pointed buds of Hybrid Tea shape open to large, double, rosettes with translucent, blush-pink petals, fading to pale creamy pink. Strong scent with a hint of lemon and fairly recurrent. Not vigorous, with a habit like that of the Hybrid Teas; leaves are large, glossy, bronzed at the margin, purple-flushed when young.

ORIGIN: 'The Friar' × 'The Friar'

'Belle Story'

David Austin, 1984   1.2 × 1.2m (4 × 4ft)

Large, rounded, double blooms, with soft pink petals incurving towards the centre, cupping a boss of golden stamens. A pleasing scent. Vigorous, well-branched shrub, with strong stems and light green leaves, blooming intermittently throughout summer. This is one of the smaller English Roses and much of its charm rests in the beautiful and unusual formation of its pretty and attractive flowers.

ORIGIN: ('Chaucer' × 'Parade') × ('The Prioress' × 'Iceberg')

'Belle Story'

'Charles Austin'

'Charles Austin'
David Austin, 1973   1.5 × 1.5m (5 × 5ft)

A tall, vigorous, and bushy plant, with large leaves. The
sumptuous blooms are carried in large, upright clusters, on
strong stems; creamy orange-apricot, paling with age. Sweet
and fruity scent. Needs hard pruning, and dead heading to
encourage it to repeat flowering.
ORIGIN: 'Chaucer' × 'Aloha'

'Charlotte'
David Austin, 1993   90 × 70cm (36 × 30in)

A recent introduction, resembling 'Graham Thomas', with perfectly rounded, double blooms, the soft yellow petals gently
incurving and neatly overlapping. Excellent Tea rose fragrance,
repeating well throughout summer. This is a vigorous, dense,
and healthy shrub.

'Chaucer'
David Austin, 1970   1.2 × 0.9m (4 × 3ft)

Obtained by crossing two once-flowering roses, 'Chaucer' is
recurrent, but with Old Rose flower form and graceful habit.
Large, deeply cupped blooms are rose pink, with a strong
fragrance of myrrh. Upright, robust and bushy, with matt, light
green leaves. It was introduced more than two decades ago and
is well established as one of the many smaller English Roses,
and famed for its magnificent display and distinctively-scented
blooms. It is ideal for planting in a scented border.
ORIGIN: 'Duchess of Montebello' × 'Constance Spry'

'Chaucer'

'Claire Rose'
David Austin, 1986

1.2 × 1m (4 × 3ft)

A lovely fully double and quartered rose, neatly cupped and packed with silky, soft blush-pink petals, ageing to white. Flowers profusely in mid-summer and repeats. A vigorous upright shrub with large, pale green leaves. Blooms tend to become spotted in warm and wet weather, affected blooms should be removed.

ORIGIN: 'Charles Austin' × (seedling × 'Iceberg')

'Claire Rose'

'Country Living'
David Austin, 1991 　　I × 1m (3 × ft)

A rose that is charming and delicate, but with a long season of bloom. A deeply cup-shaped bloom, packed tightly with short petals around a green button eye; pink fading almost to white. Compact, upright, twiggy shrub.
ORIGIN: 'Wife of Bath' × 'Graham Thomas'

'Dapple Dawn'
David Austin, 1983　　　　　　　1.5 × 1.2m (5 × 4ft)

One of the few single-flowered English Roses. Bears exceptionally large blooms, with pink petals of delicate texture, arranged around golden stamens at the centre. It is hardly scented and blooms continuously throughout summer. Best suited to informal and naturalistic plantings, an exceptionally healthy shrub.
ORIGIN: sport of 'Red Coat'

'Eglantyne'
David Austin, 1994　　　　　　I × 1m (3½ × 3ft)

A rose with large, rosette-form blooms, packed with soft, pure pink petals that curve slightly inwards. Strong, healthy bush with dense foliage.

'Dapple Dawn'

'Emmanuel'
David Austin, 1985　　　　　　2 × 1m (6 × 3ft)

Large, heavy, opulent, and intensely scented blooms, rosette-form, blush-pink with hints of gold at the base of petals, which are unusually waved and curled. An excellent, free-flowering plant, vigorous, but rather prone to blackspot.
ORIGIN: ('Chaucer' × 'Parade') × (seedling × 'Iceberg')

'Fair Bianca'
David Austin, 1982   l × lm (3 × 3ft)

An offspring of 'Belle Isis' it has strong Gallica characteristics, but the perfect formation of flower is reminiscent of a Damask; very similar to 'Mme Hardy'. Globular buds open to smallish, exquisite, crepe-textured blooms, cupped at first, later saucer-shaped with orderly ranks of creamy petals around a green eye. The fragrance is of myrrh. Low growing, upright, with light green leaves.

'Fair Bianca'

'Gertrude Jekyll'
David Austin, 1986   1.5 × lm (5 × 3ft)

The buds which slowly unfurl to very large, rosette-form, symmetrically quartered flowers of deep rich pink. Strong scent of Damask or Portland. Strong and vigorous shrub with robust stems, ample foliage and fine red thorns. Abundant and repeated flowering. Responds well to hard pruning. It can also be grown as a short climber, up to about 2.4m (8ft high). It is named after the famous English garden designer Gertrude Jekyll (1843–1932), who wrote many books about the use of garden plants, and especially their use in colour themes.
ORIGIN: 'Wife of Bath' × 'Comte de Chambord'

'Golden Celebration'
David Austin, 1992   1.2 × 1.2m (4 × 4ft)

A vigorous, rounded shrub with glossy, dark green leaves and large, cup-shaped, very double blooms of deep golden yellow, with darker tones in the petal folds. Exceptional fragrance, and has a repeat-flowering nature.

'Gertrude Jekyll'

'Graham Thomas'

David Austin, 1983 1.2 × 1.2m (4 × 4ft)

The medium-sized but full and deeply cupped blooms, of a truly Old Rose character, are of rich, glowing golden yellow, with a hint of pink at the petal base. Strong Tea rose fragrance. Upright, vigorous plant, well clothed with light green leaves.
ORIGIN: (seedling × 'Charles Austin') × (seedling × 'Iceberg')

'Heritage'

David Austin, 1984 1.2 × 1.2m (4 × 4ft)

Bears small clusters of double blooms, shell pink, a warmer tone than in 'Chaucer', and deeper pink in bud. Rich fragrance with a touch of lemon. Open, spreading shrub when young, later dense and bushy, with smooth, almost thornless stems. Repeats regularly throughout summer.
ORIGIN: seedling of English Rose × ('Wife of Bath' × 'Iceberg')

'Heritage'

'Kathryn Morley'

David Austin, 1990   75 × 60cm (30 × 24in)

A diminutive rose with dainty, cup shaped blooms, the soft pink petals are toothed at the upper margin, and gently incurved to the centre. Sweetly scented, and repeats well. A dense, bushy, and healthy little shrub. The flowers, with their delicious fragrance, contribute to the fame of this superb New English rose, which forms an ideal garden plant.

'Lucetta'

'Lucetta'

David Austin, 1983   1.5 × 1.5m (5 × 5ft)

The large, semi-double blooms are an open cup-shape, packed with soft, rounded petals, blush-pink fading almost to white, scented. Strong growth, with long, arching branches, dark foliage; continuous flowering. Can be grown as a small climber. it is one of the larger English Roses, with blooms up to 15cm (6in) across and held singly or in small bunches. It was introduced more than a decade ago and has established itself as a superb garden plant, whether in a rose border or mixed with shrubs and herbaceous perennials.

'Othello'

David Austin, 1985   1.2 × 0.9m (4 × 3ft)

An imposing rose with remarkable blooms, deeply cupped, fully-double, of a rich dark crimson, sometimes flushed purple, and becoming mauve-toned with age. Excellent Old Rose fragrance. Free-flowering and repeating reliably. Of robust constitution, tall, bushy and upright, with long, stout shoots, large, dark leaves and vicious thorns.

ORIGIN: 'Lilian Austin' × 'The Squire'

'Peach Blossom'
David Austin, 1990 1.2 × 0.9m (4 × 3ft)

A rose with the same grace, fragile delicacy and colour as peach blossom. Medium-sized, with translucent petals, flowering profusely and repeating well. The plant has been awarded a prize for fragrance by the Royal National Rose Society. Shapely, shrubby bush, which produces a good crop of hips in autumn.
ORIGIN: 'The Prioress' × 'Mary Rose'

'Perdita'
David Austin, 1983 1.2 × 0.9m (4 × 3ft)

Small, rounded, creamy buds open to shallowly cup-shaped blooms of ivory-white, intensely flushed with rich peach and apricot shades in the petal folds; fades almost to white with maturity. Strong Tea rose fragrance; awarded a prize by the Royal National Rose Society in 1984. Vigorous, well-branched, healthy and free-flowering shrub, repeating well.
ORIGIN: 'The Friar' × (seedling × 'Iceberg')

'Prospero'
David Austin, 1982 60 × 60cm (2 × 2ft)

The beauty of the old Gallicas, with many small, short petals arranged in flat, rosette-form flowers of deep crimson with mauve and purple shadings. Agreeable Old Rose fragrance. Moderate vigour, but responds well to fertile soils and feeding.
ORIGIN: 'The Knight' × 'Château de Clos Vougeot'

'Redouté'
David Austin, 1992 1.2 × 1.2m (4 × 4ft)

Large, double blooms, packed loosely with soft pink petals, are carried freely in flushes throughout summer. Light fragrance. Vigorous, healthy, well-branched shrub.

'Othello'

'Sharifa Asma'
David Austin, 1989   90 × 70cm (36 × 28in)

A rose valued for the delicacy of colour, blush-pink with yellow undertones, and the formation of blooms: shallowly cupped at first, with the inner petals arranged in a loose rosette while the outer, rounded petals reflex when fully open. Short, upright, compact bush with a rich scent.

ORIGIN: 'Mary Rose' × 'Admired Miranda'

'Sir Walter Raleigh'

'Sir Walter Raleigh'
David Austin, 1985   1.5 × 1.2m (5 × 4ft)

Exceptionally large, showy, double blooms, as much as 15cm (6in) across, much like a peony in form, and exposing a cluster of golden stamens when fully open; warm, deep pink and with excellent fragrance. Compact, tidy and bushy, with a recurrent flowering nature that ensures it remains in flower throughout most of the summer. It is named after the English adventurer and explorer Sir Walter Raleigh (1552–1618), who established a colony in Virginia, North America.

ORIGIN: 'Lilian Austin' × 'Chaucer'

'Symphony'
David Austin, 1986   1.2 × 1m (4 × 3ft)

Red-tinted in bud, opening to large, many-petalled blooms in the form of a neat rosette, reflexing when fully open: clear lemon yellow. Flowers carried in large, densely packed clusters. Prone to spotting in warm, wet weather. A reliable rose, myrrh-scented, with good foliage, freely and continuously flowering.

ORIGIN: 'The Knight' × 'Yellow Cushion'

'The Dark Lady'

David Austin, 1991 1 × 1.2m (3 × 4ft)

The large, deep cerise-crimson blooms are not perhaps as dark as the name suggests, but nevertheless, beautifully formed with many undulating petals packed into a loose rosette. Intense Old Rose fragrance. A sprawling shrub of medium height.

ORIGIN: 'Mary Rose' × 'Prospero'

'Warwick Castle'

David Austin, 1986 90 × 90cm (3 × 3ft)

Superb, double blooms with many short petals at the centre forming a flat rosette, cupped by the rounded, outer petals which reflex when fully open; glowing deep pink. Individual blooms are long-lived. Strongly scented and repeating well.

ORIGIN: 'Lilian Austin' × 'The Reeve'

'Winchester Cathedral'

David Austin, 1987 1.2 × 1.2m (4 × 4ft)

With strong Damask characteristics, very similar to its parent, but with delicate, cup-shaped, snow-white blooms, loosely packed with a mass of curled petals, and held upright on the stems. Blooms regularly throughout summer. Well-branched, bushy, and reliably healthy shrub.

ORIGIN: a sport of 'Mary Rose'

'Symphony'

SPECIES OF WILD ROSES AND THEIR HYBRIDS

Botanical species and their varieties

In addition to the multitude of complex hybrids dealt with so far, other roses – true species, and simple hybrids derived from them – have contributed much to our gardens as shrubs or climbers.

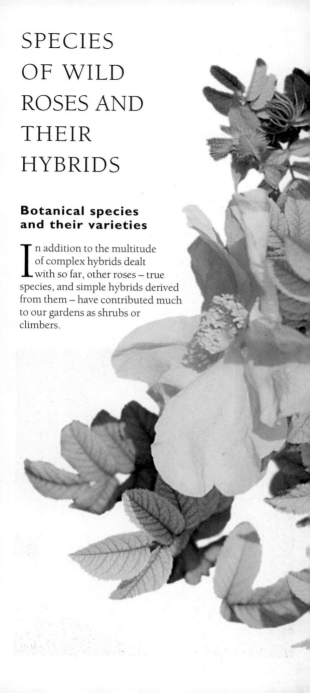

Many are the fruits of the introductions by the great plant collectors in the 19th century, perhaps especially appreciated when William Robinson extolled the virtues of a more natural style of gardening in reaction to the geometric excesses of the Victorian period. They gave rise to varieties which were often possessed of the vigour that is commonly seen in wild species, and many have passed the test of time. The most prolific of species among the shrub roses is *Rosa rugosa*, and among the most familiar of these are the Rugosa hybrids created at the beginning of the century, the Grootendorsts, from crosses with *R. multiflora*. Interesting varieties also come from *Rosa pimpinellifolia* and *Rosa rubiginosa* (syn. *Rosa eglanteria*). There are fewer simple hybrids derived from the climbing or rambling species, although there are amongst them some of great beauty. They include: *Rosa banksiae*, *R. bracteata*, *R. laevigata*, *R. setigera*, and *R. xanthina*. With the exception of *R. setigera* and *R. xanthina*, none of these roses are fully hardy, and the same applies to the forms and hybrids which are derived from them.

Rosa × micrugosa

ROSA RUBIGINOSA HYBRIDS

The sweet briars

Rosa rubiginosa (syn. *R. eglanteria*) is a widespread native of both Asia and Europe, and is perhaps the most romantic of all wild roses. It is the English Sweet Briar – Shakespeare's eglantine of *A Midsummer Night's Dream*:

> I know a bank whereon the wild thyme blows,
> Where oxlips and the nodding violet grows
> Quite over-canopied with luscious woodbine,
> With sweet musk-roses, and with eglantine.

R. rubiginosa is particularly valuable for its fragrance – not only of its flowers, but for the apple-like scent of its leaves, especially strong after rain, or when crushed. Although they generally need little pruning, Peter Beales suggests clipping annually so as to encourage the growth of new shoots which emit a stronger scent. A dense, branching shrub with arching branches, it bears single blooms, solitary or in clusters of up to 7, varying from pale to deep pink, followed by ovoid, or almost globose, bright red hips, which persist well into

Rosa foetida

Rosa foetida 'Persiana'

winter. Similar to, but less vigorous than the Dog Rose, *R. canina*, it has deciduous leaves, with 5–9 ovate leaflets, neatly veined and toothed, dark green, and downy and glandular beneath.

Towards the end of the 18th century, several *R. rubiginosa* hybrids appeared on the scene, amongst them 'Manning's Blush' (1797) still grown today but with blooms more like those of a Tea rose. It was not until the end of the 19th century that the sweet briar began to assert itself, notably in the creation of the Penzance Briars. Lord Penzance was tempted away from the legal profession by his love of roses and added to the by now lengthy list of varieties a delightful group of hybrids, which derive mainly from crosses using Bourbons, Hybrid Perpetuals, *Rosa foetida* (Austrian Briar), *R. foetida* 'Bicolor' (Austrian Copper Briar), and *R. foetida* 'Persiana' (Persian Double Yellow).

The Sweet Briars flower once only at the beginning of summer, and although they may later bear beautiful hips, they have little to offer for the remainder of the year. They are suitable for the wilder areas of the garden, certainly in informal areas, and many are useful as hedging and in hedgerows. They make few demands in cultivation, are robust and healthy, and need little pruning other than to confine them to bounds.

'Amy Robsart'

Lord Penzance, Great Britain, 1894   3.5 × 2.5m (11 × 8ft)

Vigorous, arching bush with smallish leaves, spectacular when in flower in early summer. Bears a single flush of slightly perfumed, almost single blooms of glowing pink, paler at the centre, around the crown of golden stamens. Sometimes reluctant to fruit. Foliage only slightly fragrant. Tolerant of poor soils and shade.

ORIGIN: *Rosa rubiginosa* × a Hybrid Perpetual or a Bourbon

Rosa foetida 'Bicolor'

'Greenmantle'
Lord Penzance, Great Britain, 1895 2.5 × 1.5m (8 × 5ft)

Not well known but deserving attention, has single rosy-pink
blooms with a white eye and prominent yellow stamens. Very
aromatic leaves on a tall vigorous shrub.

'Hebe's Lip'
('Reine Blanche', 'Rubrotincta')
William Paul, Great Britain, 1912 1.2 × 1.2m (4 × 4ft)

A very old rose, sometimes classified among the Damasks.
Dainty buds open to cupped, single blooms, white, flushed
deep pink at the petal rim, and with a strong scent of musk.
They close at night. A vigorous shrub of open habit, with
many strongly down-curved thorns, and rather coarse but
very aromatic leaves. Fruits well in autumn.
ORIGIN: probably a Damask × *Rosa rubiginosa*

'Janet's Pride'
('Clementine')
William Paul, Great Britain, 1892 1.2 × 1.2m (4 × 4ft)

A very interesting wild form, said to have been found in a hedge
in Cheshire, and welcomed for its scented, delicate, semi-
double blooms, ivory at the centre grading to brilliant pink at
the edge of petals, and fading to a translucent dusky pink. A
slender shrub, with few thorns and robust, finely-toothed,
slightly aromatic leaves. The origination of this rose is not clear;
although it was introduced by W. Paul and Sons in 1892, Mr
Shepard tells that it was earlier known as 'Clementine'. Other
reports say that it was found growing wild in a Cheshire lane.
ORIGIN: ? *R. damascena* × *R. rubiginosa*

'Julia Mannering'
Lord Penzance, Great Britain, 1895 1.8 × 1.2m (6 × 4ft)

A tall, robust shrub which deserves to be better known, but is
difficult to acquire. Blooms are large, almost single and pearly
pink, veined darker pink, carried along the length of the
branches in early summer. Leaves aromatic, small and dark
green, creating an attractive background for the flowers.

'Lady Penzance'
Lord Penzance, Great Britain, 1894 2.2 × 1.8m (7 × 6ft)

This splendid rose owes its popularity to the brilliant coppery
salmon-pink of its delicate, single blooms. Dense, vigorous
shrub, with orange-red hips in autumn. Leaves small, mid-
green, aromatic. The flowers are said to have a fragrance
reminiscent of *Rosa foetida*, the Austrian Yellow and parent of
many roses.
ORIGIN: *Rosa rubiginosa* × *Rosa foetida* 'Bicolor'

'Lady Penzance'

'Lord Penzance'

Lord Penzance, Great Britain, c. 1890   1.8 × 1.8 (6 × 6ft)

Buff-yellow blooms, tinted pink and lemon-yellow at the centre, of a beautiful delicate texture, followed by brilliant red hips in autumn. Both flowers and foliage are sweetly scented; a rose of great beauty for the wild garden. A fairly vigorous and very thorny shrub.

ORIGIN: *Rosa rubiginosa* × 'Harrison's Yellow' (derived from *R. foetida*)

'Manning's Blush'

c. 1894   1.5 × 1.2m (5 × 4ft)

A very old rose of unknown origin, may have been in cultivation at the end of the 18th century. A hybrid of *R. rubiginosa*, with unusual blooms in its group: flat and double, scented, very soft pink, fading to white. Occasionally produces a few blooms in autumn. Rather compact, rounded shrub, with abundant, small and aromatic leaves.

'Meg Merrilees'

Lord Penzance, Great Britain, c. 1890   2.5 × 2m (8 × 6ft)

One of the favourite Hybrid Sweet Briars, with bright crimson, sweetly scented blooms displaying a tuft of golden stamens; bears a good crop of red hips in autumn. Very vigorous, very thorny and with strongly scented leaves. Suitable for hedging.

ORIGIN: probably a cross between *Rosa rubiginosa* and a Hybrid Perpetual or a Bourbon

'Lord Penzance'

ROSA PIMPINELLIFOLIA HYBRIDS

Hybrid Scots Briars, the Burnet roses

The name *pimpinellifolia* is thought to be a reference to the imagined similarity of the small, delicate leaves to those of the pimpernels (*Anagallis* species); many know the Burnet rose affectionately as the prickly rose, and *Rosa pimpinellifolia* is indeed densely clothed in straight, slender thorns and bristles; its older botanical name *R. spinosissima*, meaning most spiny, is more descriptive. It is extremely widespread, in Europe, SW and C Asia, east to China and Korea, but above all in northern coastal regions; it thrives even in very poor, sandy soils, on dunes and heathlands, from Scotland to Siberia. Various forms exist: the species has single, creamy white blooms, creamy yellow in *R. pimpinellifolia* 'Hispida', and larger, and creamy white in *R. pimpinellifolia* 'Grandiflora' (syn. 'Altaica'). Given its native habitats, it is not surprising that these are amongst the hardiest of roses, resistant to gales, storms, snow and frost. In addition to their beautiful foliage and flowers, the Pimpinellifolias offer extremely decorative hips, large and spherical, and ranging from deep red to dark chocolate brown and black.

These very thorny roses owe their presence in gardens initially to Robert Brown of Perth, who collected specimens from the wild, and following careful breeding and selection, introduced a substantial number of hybrids; as many as two hundred were listed. Whilst the wild species is a rather low, suckering shrub with usually single, creamy blooms, the varieties created were more diverse: they bear double or semi-double blooms in profusion along the length of the prickly stems – with colours ranging from cream to yellow, and with all shades of pink and purple – although all retain the simple delicacy of the species. The autumn hips are almost invariably impressive, and very ornamental. Among the first varieties the following deserve a mention: 'Double White' (still alive and thriving), 'Double Cream', 'Double Blush', 'Double Yellow'.

Burnet Roses or Scotch Roses were very popular in Great Britain but less so in the rest of Europe. They remain, in fact, better suited to northern climates, and have only one brief but very beautiful burst of bloom in early summer. Thus their success was limited and many varieties have disappeared from cultivation. Nevertheless, one variety had the qualities necessary to become one of the world's most popular and widely grown roses, perhaps unrivalled in grace and delicacy: 'Stanwell Perpetual'.

Scotch Roses were destined to enjoy another moment of glory in the middle years of the 20th century. In Germany, in the nurseries of W. Kordes, a new group of roses were created from crosses of the Burnet rose with Hybrid Teas.

Pimpinellifolia hybrids are amongst the least demanding of roses, they grow in almost any soil, and are almost without exception, healthy, vigorous and disease resistant. They need very little pruning, other than the occasional removal of the oldest stems at the base in winter so that they may be replaced by vigorous new growth.

Hips of *Rosa pimpinellifolia*

'Andrewsii'

c. 1806

1.2 × 0.9m (4 × 3ft)

Bears numerous, very pretty, semi-double blooms of rosy red and cream, with yellow stamens, in late spring/early summer, with a second flush later in the season. Thorny and well-foliated shrub, fully hardy, suitable for really cold climates. It is sometimes known as Andrew's Rose.

'Dunwich Rose'

60 × 120cm (2 × 4ft)

Probably a very old variety, rediscovered in the 1950s at Dunwich, in Suffolk. A low-growing, creeping bush, notable for its early flowering and procumbent habit, possessing all the characteristics of a true pimpinellifolia, the pretty leaves, and the numerous, needle-like prickles included. Bears very attractive, small, single blooms of lemon-yellow, followed by a good crop of hips in autumn.

Rosa pimpinellifolia 'Double White'

'Mrs Colville'

1.2 × 0.9m (4 × 3ft)

Bears single, crimson blooms with a white eye and prominent yellow stamens, followed by elongated hips which suggest *R. pendulina* parentage. Thorny branches, dark red-brown in colour, bear plentiful small, dark and graceful leaves.
ORIGIN: probably a cross between *Rosa pimpinellifolia* and *Rosa pendulina*

Rosa pimpinellifolia 'Double White'

1.5 × 1.2m (5 × 4ft)

Bears numerous dainty, double blooms, the pure white petals incurved to give a globular shape, almost obscuring the golden stamens. They have a very pleasant lily-of-the-valley fragrance. A dense, rounded bush, vigorous, very hardy, and with an abundance of delicate, almost fern-like foliage.

'Stanwell Perpetual'

Robert Brown, Great Britain, 1838   1.5 × 1.5m (5 × 5ft)

Gertrude Jekyll gives credit for this very special rose to Brown, but its origin is not certain as frequently it is suggested it was found as a chance seedling in a garden at Stanwell. However, it is certain that it was put on the market by the nursery of Lee and Kennedy at Hammersmith, London. A very graceful rose whose delicate appearance belies its robust constitution and hardiness. Along the length of its arching stems, it bears small, blush-pink blooms, flat, fully double and quartered, often with a little button eye; sweetly scented, and with a long flowering period, in repeated flushes from late spring to autumn in good conditions, peaking in mid-summer. The leaves, typical of the *pimpinellifolia* in shape, are small, grey-green, and sometimes flushed with purple. The slender, arching branches tend to wander, but seldom need support, since the bush will form a self-supporting mound: alternatively grow in groups of three, as Miss Jekyll recommends, so that each sustains the other.

ORIGIN: *Rosa damascena* × *Rosa pimpinellifolia*

'William III'

90 × 90cm (3 × 3ft)

An exquisite rose with small, semi-double blooms, in late spring/early summer; dark crimson in colour, later assuming magenta tones, sweetly scented. Bears a splendid display of chocolate brown, almost black, rounded hips in autumn. Tidy in habit, and densely suckering, it bears an abundance of delicate, grey-green leaves.

'Stanwell Perpetual'

ROSA RUGOSA

Rosa rugosa 'Kamtchactika'

Rosa rugosa, the Japanese or Turkestan rose, which the Japanese call Ramanas, has appeared in Oriental paintings for many centuries. It arrived in Europe quite late – in 1796 according to the writer Ellen Willmott – although it appears to have been forgotten or overlooked and is next seen in 1845, described in Nicholson's authoritative *Illustrated Dictionary of Gardening*, published between 1884 and 1888.

It is native not only to Japan but also to northern China, Siberia and Korea; extremely robust, thorny and resistant to cold, it could be described as the Burnet Rose of the East. It has naturalised in the northern regions of Europe and, due to its resistance to the elements, is frequently used (in Scandinavia, for example) to form magnificent boundary hedges, even in the cities, an indication of its noted tolerance of urban pollution.

The species hybridises readily, often spontaneously, and has given rise to many different forms: given its robustness, it has often been used as a rootstock for grafting. The species is a large, vigorous shrub with single, bright pink-purple blooms, having light but pleasing fragrance, and giving rise to very conspicuous, rounded hips in scarlet and bright orange. The leaves are a very attractive bright green, wrinkled, as the specific epithet implies, and with prominent, deeply impressed veins; they frequently take on autumn tints of purple and gold, in beautiful contrast to the brilliantly coloured, and often large, hips.

The species is grown less frequently than its forms and hybrids, which include the very beautiful *R. rugosa* 'Alba', a compact shrub about one metre (3ft) in height, with large, single, silky blooms of dazzling white. The purple-crimson *R. rugosa* 'Rubra' is also very attractive. As blooms are carried in flushes throughout summer and autumn, they produce effects which are uncommon in the roses – the simultaneous bearing of fruit and flower.

Towards the end of the 19th century, renewed interest in the species led to the creation of a range of Rugosa hybrids which have become some of the most popular of modern garden shrubs. The beauty of the leaves, the repeat-flowering, in combination with vigour, disease-resistance, and above all, adaptability to almost any soil make them valuable in a range of locations. Although most retain the simple elegance of the species, bearing single, semi-double or double blooms, they have a much extended colour range, and are frequently highly scented; the fragrance of a Rugosa hedge will carry for considerable distances.

The first group of hybrids asserted itself at the end of the 19th century, but many were also created in the 20th: amongst these, it is impossible to omit 'Agnes', repeat-flowering, with a very fruity scent, and one of the few with yellow blooms; 'Sara Van Fleet', strongly fragrant, of a translucent pale pink; 'Thérèse Burgnet', a splendid magenta, and 'Scabrosa', introduced in 1960 by Harkness, exceptional for its enormous, strawberry-pink blooms, and large fruit.

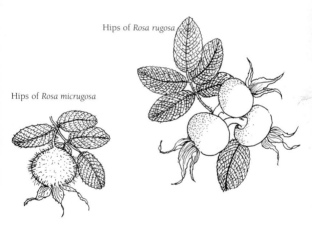

Hips of *Rosa rugosa*

Hips of *Rosa micrugosa*

Rugosa roses can be grown in almost any soil and situation, and are extremely useful as hedging, particularly in coastal regions. They must have ample room to spread; many will make a hedge to 1.2m (4ft) across, or more. They need little pruning: hedges can be cut back by about one third in winter, if necessary, to confine to bounds; the occasional removal of old wood, by cutting back to the base, will keep them well-furnished to ground level. Specimen shrubs will also respond well to cutting back of side shoots by about one third in winter.

'Belle Poitevine'

G. Bruant, France, 1894   1.8 × 1.5m (6 × 5ft)

Pointed, elegant buds open to large, semi-double blooms,
mauve-pink, opening almost flat, but with little scent. Repeat-
flowering, from early summer to autumn. Plentiful, typical
rugosa leaves, deeply veined and bright green, turning gold and
bronze in autumn when the shrub displays large, brilliant
orange-red hips.

'Blanc Double de Coubert'

Cochet-Cochet, Coubert, France, 1892   1.5 × 1.2m (5 × 4ft)

The jewel of the group, deservedly popular for the beautiful,
double blooms of a pure, snow-white, and a sugary fragrance
reminiscent of violets. A free-flowering shrub, but often reluctant to fruit. 'Souvenir de Philemon Cochet', not widely grown,
is a sport with very double blooms, white tinged pink, with narrow, curled petals at the centre; very free-flowering.
ORIGIN: *Rosa rugosa* × 'Sombreuil'

'Conrad Ferdinand Meyer'

F. Müller, Germany, 1899   3 × 2.5m (10 × 8ft)

Large, double, cupped blooms, almost of a Hybrid Tea shape, in
unfading silvery pink; strongly perfumed. Blooms profusely
from early summer to autumn; one of the earliest to flower. A
vigorous, stout-stemmed shrub with rather coarse foliage. Its
sport 'Nova Zembla' has pure white blooms; introduced in Great
Britain by Mees in 1907.
ORIGIN: *R. rugosa* 'Germanica' × ('Gloire de Dijon' × 'Duc de
Rohan')

'Fimbriata'
('Phoebe's Frilled Pink',
'Dianthiflora')

Morlet, France, 1891   1.2 × 1.2m (4 × 4ft)

Very unusual with its small clusters of semi-double, pink-tinted,
white flowers, which have conspicuously fringed petal tips,
rather like those of the clove pinks, *Dianthus*. Well-scented, and
repeating reliably from early summer to autumn.
ORIGIN: *Rosa rugosa* × 'Mme Alfred Carrière'

'F. J. Grootendorst'

De Goey, Holland, 1918   1.2 × 0.9m (4 × 3ft)

The first of a robust and useful family, the Grootendorsts, bearing clusters of small, double blooms, crimson, and with frilled
petal margins; unfortunately little scent, but a vigorous, upright
shrub with bright green, deeply-veined leaves. 'Pink
Grootendorst', introduced in 1923, is pale pink, and there is a
white sport too, 'White Grootendorst', introduced in 1962.
ORIGIN: *Rosa rugosa* 'Rubra' × 'Mme Norbert Levavasseur'

'Blanc Double de Coubert'

'Frau Dagmar Hastrup'
('Frau Dagmar Hartopp')

Hastrup, Germany, 1914   80 × 120cm (2½ × 4ft)

A compact and low-growing hybrid of uncertain origin, very useful for hedging. Bears large, single blooms of translucent, silvery pink, followed by glossy, tomato-red hips. The graceful *rugosa*-type leaves are apple-green.

'Hansa'

Schaum & Van Tol, Holland, 1905   1.2 × 0.9m (4 × 3ft)

A free-flowering shrub with large, full, red-violet blooms with a strong, spicy, clove-like fragrance. Bears flowers and large, red hips concurrently.

'Conrad Ferdinand Meyer'

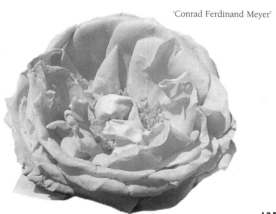

'Mrs Anthony Waterer'

'Lady Curzon'

Turner, Great Britain, 1901 2.5 × 2.5m (8 × 8ft)

Bears very large, single flowers, of silky texture; soft, translucent pink shading to white at the centre, with a prominent boss of golden stamens. A dense, vigorous, bushy shrub, which will climb with support, but is very useful as ground cover if allowed to sprawl. Good scent, but with a short blooming season, over about three weeks in early summer.

ORIGIN: *Rosa macrantha* × *Rosa rugosa* 'Rubra'

'Mrs Anthony Waterer'

Waterer, Great Britain, 1898 1.5 × 1.5m (5 × 5ft)

An old variety, with well-shaped, semi-double blooms, bright crimson, and well-scented; blooms profusely in early summer, and occasionally bears a lesser flush in autumn. A vigorous and wide-spreading bush.

ORIGIN: 'Général Jacqueminot' × *Rugosa* hybrid

'Parfum de l'Hay'

Jules Gravereaux, France, 1901 1.5 × 0.9m (5 × 3ft)

Globular buds open to large, flat and double blooms of a rich cherry-red which assume purple tones in warm weather. The fragrance is good but not as strong as in 'Roseraie de l'Hay'. A bushy, thorny shrub, with dark leaves, flowering reliably over a long season. It is an ideal variety for hot climates and grows well in California.

ORIGIN: (*Rosa* × *damascena* × 'Général Jacqueminot') × *Rosa rugosa*

'Roseraie de l'Hay'

Cochet-Cochet, France, 1901

1.8 × 1.5m (6 × 5ft)

An old favourite, much loved for the opulence of the large, delightfully scented, crimson-purple blooms. Of unknown parentage, it bears the name of the famous, and still thriving, rose garden of Jules Gravereaux, south of Paris. Created by him in 1910, with the intention of collecting all the roses cultivated by Empress Josephine. It bears very large, semi-double blooms, opening flat, with a fragrance of sugared almonds. A robust, vigorous shrub, well-clothed in bright green leaves, flowering throughout summer, and with good autumn colour.

'Schneezwerg' ('Snow Dwarf')

Peter Lambert, Germany, 1912

1.5 × 1.2m (5 × 4ft)

Small, semi-double, well-shaped blooms of pure white, with golden stamens, are carried throughout summer and autumn, in fine contrast with the tomato-red hips. Well-scented, long, reliable blooming; a robust and dense shrub, with glossy, grey-tinted leaves, well-suited to hedging.

ORIGIN: *Rosa rugosa × R. bracteata*

'Roseraie de l'Hay'

Rosa × *microrugosa*
Prior to 1905   2 × 1.2m (6 × 4ft)

A lovely cross, taking the best from both parents: beautiful,
wrinkled leaves and decorative prickles from *Rosa rugosa*, delicate flowers from *Rosa roxburghii*, of a pale, pearly pink, not
profuse but carried over a long period. Bears very attractive
fruits, globose, red-brown, and covered in a mass of long, stiff
bristles. A vigorous shrub, with stout stems, very useful as
dense, impenetrable hedging. There is a form with darker
blooms. *R. microrugosa* 'Alba' has pure white flowers.
ORIGIN: *Rosa rugosa* × *Rosa roxburghii*

Rosa × *paulii*   *Rosa* × *paulii* 'Rosea'

Rosa × *paulii*
Prior to 1903   0.8 × 3m (2½ × 10ft)

Discovered in the garden of Strasbourg Botanical Institute at the
beginning of the century. A trailing species, with very thorny
stems, and dark, leathery leaves, long used as ground cover,
beneath shrubs, or to clothe sunny banks. The stems grow up to
about 4m (12ft) long and lie flat on the ground. Bears single
blooms that are notable for the well-spaced, elongated white
petals; fragrant but only once-blooming.
ORIGIN: *Rosa rugosa* × *Rosa arvensis*

Rosa × *paulii* 'Rosea'
Prior to 1912   0.8 × 3m (2½ × 10ft)

At mid-summer the rose is almost hidden under the mass of
deep pink blooms; similar to *R.* × *paulii*, but with more serrated
petals and darker stems and leaves.
ORIGIN: sport of *Rosa* × *paulii*

ROSA BANKSIAE

The Banksian rose

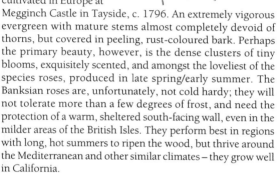

A climbing species, native to rocky areas in the mountains of central and western China, and first cultivated in Europe at Megginch Castle in Tayside, c. 1796. An extremely vigorous evergreen with mature stems almost completely devoid of thorns, but covered in peeling, rust-coloured bark. Perhaps the primary beauty, however, is the dense clusters of tiny blooms, exquisitely scented, and amongst the loveliest of the species roses, produced in late spring/early summer. The Banksian roses are, unfortunately, not cold hardy; they will not tolerate more than a few degrees of frost, and need the protection of a warm, sheltered south-facing wall, even in the milder areas of the British Isles. They perform best in regions with long, hot summers to ripen the wood, but thrive around the Mediterranean and other similar climates – they grow well in California.

Create a permanent framework by tying-in to wires as growth proceeds. As plants reach maturity, prune out the oldest wood immediately after flowering, to reduce over-crowding and to allow light and air to young replacement growth. Any long growth produced during summer must be tied-in to the wall before the onset of winter frosts. Tip back frost damaged growth in spring.

Rosa banksiae var. banksiae (Rosa banksiae 'Alba Plena')

1807   4 × 2.5m (12 × 8ft) or more

Found in a garden in Canton by William Kerr, in 1807, and sent to Sir Joseph Banks, then director at Kew. A rampant, thornless climber, with smooth, golden brown bark, which peels when mature, and light green leaves. The small, clustered blooms are double, rosette-form, creamy white, and with a delicious fragrance of violets, carried in late spring/early summer. Perhaps seen at its magnificent best on the pergolas of the gardens of the Riviera. Of all the forms of *Rosa banksiae*, this is by far the most popular and commonly grown type in North America.

Rosa banksiae 'Lutea'
c. 1825   6 × 3m (20 × 10ft)

Said to be the hardiest form and growing well in the Cambridge
Botanic Gardens. Introduced by J. D. Parks from China, in
1824, a very vigorous climber with large clusters of small, very
double, butter yellow blooms in late spring. The best known of
the group, and the most likely to thrive in temperate climates
such as that in Britain.

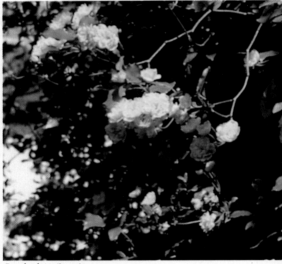
Rosa banksiae 'Lutea'

Rosa banksiae 'Lutescens'
1870   6 × 3m (20 × 10ft)

Introduced from China, and perhaps grown first at Daniel
Hanbury's gardens at La Mortola, Ventimiglia; sent from there to
Kew. Bears single blooms, slightly larger than in 'Lutea'; yellow,
and very fragrant, in late spring. Leaves are semi-evergreen,
stems thornless. Not hardy.

Rosa × *fortuneana*
1850   3.5 × 3.5m (11 × 11ft)

Unknown in the wild, of garden origin in China. Less vigorous
than *R. banksiae*, and equally frost tender. The dark green stems
bear thin-textured evergreen leaves, and solitary, large, double
blooms, to 10cm (4in) across; pure white and fragrant. In Italy it
was used as an understock (rootstock).
ORIGIN: it is widely thought to be a cross between *Rosa banksiae* and *Rosa laevigata*

ROSA BRACTEATA

Native to SE China and Taiwan, and naturalised in the warmer regions of the eastern United States, it is known as the Macartney Rose following its introduction to Europe by Lord Macartney in 1793, on his return from a diplomatic visit. A vigorous, evergreen or semi-evergreen climber with long, dull brown stems, armed with paired, hooked thorns and bristles. The leaves are attractive, with 5–11 elliptic to oblong leaflets, glossy bright green above, and downy beneath. The blooms, up to 10cm (4in) across, are very distinctive: single, pure white, with golden stamens, and a richly fruity fragrance, they have large, downy, deeply toothed bracts beneath. It flowers continuously from early summer until the first frosts, but even in milder areas of Britain, needs the protection of a warm sheltered south-facing wall. In warmer regions, it makes a splendid free-standing specimen. Needs little or no pruning.

In 1799, plants reached North America and were sent to Thomas Jefferson at Monticello. Later it become established in warm regions and has been used to prevent soil erosion in some southern States. This is because its long, underground stems and shoots unify soil.

'Mermaid'

William Paul, Great Britain, 1917 9 × 6m (28 × 20ft)

An old favourite, needing a warm, sheltered position to thrive. Extremely vigorous, with distinctive, dark brown stems clothed in vicious thorns, and glossy, rich green leaves which are evergreen or semi-evergreen; it may be cut to the base by frosts in severe winters. The blooms are exceptionally beautiful, very fragrant, and carried from mid-summer to autumn: very large, single, saucer-shaped, and lemon yellow with a prominent ring of deep golden-orange stamens. It does not transplant well, and usually is extremely slow to become established, but thereafter needs little or no pruning. Young wood is brittle, so ensure all shoots are tied to their supports, especially in autumn.
ORIGIN: *Rosa bracteata* × a yellow Tea rose

ROSA
BRUNONII

'La Mortola'

The Himalayan Musk rose, native to northern India, the Himalaya and Nepal, introduced c.1822. A vigorous climber reaching 7m (22ft), with grey-green stems, flushed rose-brown when young, and clothed in short, stout, hooked thorns. The leaves are blue-green, and downy. Bears single, creamy, strongly scented flowers in conical clusters in early summer. Needs a sunny, sheltered position to bloom well. 'La Mortola', grown in the Hanbury Gardens in Ventimiglia, Italy, is similar, perhaps more tender, and with more downy leaves.

'Paul's Himalayan Musk'

'Paul's Himalayan Musk'

William Paul, end 19th century   6 × 3.5m (20 × 11ft)

Of uncertain origin, but most probably a seedling of *Rosa brunonii*. A robust and healthy climber, with pliable stems clothed in broad, hooked thorns, reaching up to 9m (28ft) in good conditions. In mid-summer, bears large, cascading trusses of small, double, rosette-form blooms, white, flushed with delicate lilac-pink, and sweetly fragrant.

'Rosa Dupontii'

'Rosa Dupontii'

Dupont c. 1817   2.2 × 1.8m (7 × 6ft)

Robust, with lax but not climbing stems and large, very fragrant, pure white flowers amid matt grey-green leaves. It is one of the least thorny of roses and certainly one of the most beautiful. It is thought to be a cross between *Rosa damascena* and *R. moschata*. 'Rosa Dupontii' is named after M. Dupont, the founder of the rose gardens at Luxembourg, Paris. He was commissioned by the Empress Josephine to assist her in assembling a collection of roses for planting in her world-famous garden at La Malmaison, on the outskirts of Paris.

ROSA LAEVIGATA

'Anemone' ('Anemonoides')

Although native from South China to Burma, it has naturalised in the southern United States of America,
where it was introduced c. 1759, and has become
known there as the Cherokee Rose, and adopted as the state
flower of Georgia. A vigorous, evergreen climber, to 10m
(33ft) or more, with green stems clothed in stout, scattered
thorns. It seldom thrives anywhere in the UK, needing long,
hot summers to ripen wood sufficiently to bloom well; a rose
for warm continental or Mediterranean-type climates. This is
a shame, because it bears splendid, well-scented, pure white,
single blooms, with very large, rounded petals that narrow at
the base, and perch gracefully on top of red peduncles. It
blooms in late spring/early summer. The foliage is a very pretty shining green, with 3 small, ovate or lanceolate
leaflets, and in suitable conditions it bears large,
prickly, egg-shaped hips, yellow at first, brown
when ripe. They are very attractive.

'Ramona'

'Anemone' ('Anemonoides')

J. C. Schmidt, Germany, 1896   4 × 1m (12 × 3ft)

A rose with many drawbacks, little scent, once-blooming, scanty leaves, awkward habit, and tenderness (though hardier than the species). One forgives everything for the surprisingly large, delicate, papery blooms of a rich pink, paling at the centre, around glistening golden stamens. Needs a warm, sunny, sheltered wall, or will scramble through an old tree. Associates well with a procumbent rose, like *Rosa × paulii*. In North America it is known as the Pink Cherokee or Anemone Rose.

ORIGIN: probably a cross between *Rosa laevigata* and a Tea Rose

'Ramona'

Dietrich & Turner, USA, 1913   4 × 1m (12 × 3ft)

A sport of 'Anemone', from California, very similar to its parent, with all its drawbacks, but with bright red-pink blooms, with a pale pink reverse. May repeat in autumn, and said to be hardier than the variety 'Anemone'. In North America this rose is widely known as the Red Cherokee.

'Silver Moon'

Van Fleet, USA, 1910   6 × 2.5m (20 × 8ft)

A climbing rose with plentiful glossy, leathery leaves and lush growth; needs a warm, sunny position to bloom well. Bears clusters of large, semi-double, creamy white blooms, tinted amber at the petal base, and with deep golden stamens. Good apple-like fragrance. A vigorous and interesting rose, fairly hardy.

ORIGIN: *Rosa laevigata* × (*Rosa wichuraiana* × 'Devoniensis')

'Silver Moon'

135

ROSA SETIGERA

'Baltimore Belle'

The Prairie Rose, native to the great prairies of North America, from the Great Lakes to Texas and Florida, and introduced to Europe in 1810. A large shrub with long, slender, trailing or rambling stems, and deciduous, dark green leaves with 3–5 ovate, pointed, and coarsely toothed leaflets. It bears small corymbs of single blooms, deep pink, fading to white with a neat central cluster of golden stamens, and is one of the latest to bloom, in mid to late summer, thereafter producing small, rounded, red hips. The American horticulturists of the first half of the 19th century used *R. setigera* in the creation of a small number of climbers, valued for cold resistance and late flowering.

'Baltimore Belle'

Samuel Feast, USA, 1843   5 × 2m (15 × 6ft)

A favourite of 19th century gardens, now rather neglected, a rambler with an abundance of glossy leaves, and clusters of very pretty, double blooms of soft blush-pink to rosy white. Pleasing fragrance, and very disease resistant. Shows some similarity to *Rosa sempervirens* hybrids. This rose has also been used as an understock (rootstock) when budding roses.

ORIGIN: *Rosa setigera* × a Noisette

'Erinnerung an Brod' ('Souvenir de Brod')

Geschwind, Hungary, 1886   3.5 × 2m (11 × 6ft)

Sometimes included with the Hybrid Perpetuals, and widely used in breeding. Bears large, very double, quartered blooms of rich cerise, that fade to magenta and purple; very fragrant.

ROSE XANTHINA

N ative to northern China and to Korea, and introduced into Europe in 1906, a large, upright shrub which may reach three metres (10ft) in height. The brown stems bear broad-based thorns, and dark green leaves with 7–13 small, rounded leaflets, and in spring, small, semi-double, yellow blooms on short stalks. Although a very attractive species, more commonly seen as the well-known clone 'Canary Bird'.

'Canary Bird'

'Canary Bird'

1907
2.5 × 2m (8 × 6ft)

A large shrub or small climber, with stout chocolate-brown stems bearing many arching laterals clothed along their length in fragrant, brilliant canary yellow flowers. Elegant foliage, small, grey-green and fern-like. Flowers once in late spring, and then carries an abundance of large, dark purple hips. Needs a warm, sunny position in light, well-drained soil. May be cut back by hard frost but usually re-sprouts from the base. It has received many awards, and is thought to have been raised at Osterley Park, England.

ORIGIN: probably a cross between *Rosa xanthina* f. *spontanea* and *Rosa xanthina* f. *hugonis*

RAMBLING
ROSES

The distinction between ramblers and climbers is one that has led to much confusion, although, in essence, the difference is very simple. The ramblers produce long, flexible stems from the base of the plant in summer, and these bear clusters of 3–21 small blooms along their length during the following summer. They have then served their purpose in gardens, and the flowered shoots are cut out at the base immediately after flowering. The climbers, on the other hand, may go on to produce wood that blooms for several to many

'Félicité et Perpétue'

years, on short laterals arising from the main branches; many are remontant and will bear their large flowers singly or in small clusters. Once they have been trained to produce a framework, only the laterals are cut back, to within 3–4 buds of the main framework. Most of the climbers derive from varieties with *R. moschata*, *R. chinensis*, and *R. gigantea* in their genetic make up, and examples of these will be found throughout the preceding text; many of the varieties described have climbing sports.

There are three main groups of rambling roses, derived from *Rosa multiflora*, *Rosa sempervirens* and *Rosa wichuraiana* and the closely related *R. luciae*. A small group of ramblers, the Ayrshire Roses, were derived from *Rosa arvensis*; well-known and appreciated in the past, they are, unfortunately, no longer widely grown.

The ramblers bloom only once, usually in early or mid-summer, although they may do so over relatively long periods, and the best do so with spectacular abandon. Their flexible stems are especially suitable for training on walls, pergolas, pillars and arbours, for clothing old or moribund trees.

MULTIFLORA RAMBLERS

Rosa *multiflora*, syn. *R. polyantha*, native to northern China, Korea and Japan, arrived in Europe at the beginning of the 19th century. It is naturalised in the United States of America. It is a vigorous species with arching, trailing or climbing stems, producing annual shoots up to 3m (10ft) in length, bearing slender, straight prickles, usually in pairs, and leaves with 5–11

Rosa multiflora 'Carnea'

leaflets. It flowers on the previous season's wood in early summer, bearing pyramidal clusters of small, white flowers, very similar to those of the bramble, with a sweet, delicate fragrance, which are followed by small, red, oval hips. There are several interesting forms including 'Carnea', with double, rosette-form blooms in soft flesh-pink, and 'Grevillei', the Seven Sisters Rose, with large clusters of blooms in a range of (seven) colours, from deep pink-purple fading to white.

During the 19th century several hybrid forms were successful; in particular 'De la Grifferaie', a variety created in Japan and subsequently utilised in hybridisation, and 'Russelliana', the Old Spanish Rose, which was very popular in Victorian cottage gardens. But it was only towards the end of the 19th century that *Rosa multiflora* made a name for itself in the history of the rose, playing two important but very different roles. The first was as a parent of the Polyanthas in the nurseries of Guillot, and later, of Sisley, near Paris; these, after the customary processes of complex crossings, gave rise to the Floribundas, which, with the Hybrid Teas, are the most widely grown of Modern roses. The second role was that played in the creation, mainly thanks to the work of William Paul, of a series of very interesting rambler roses, some of which, such as 'Goldfinch' and 'The Garland' are among today's most commonly grown ramblers. They are among the most beautiful ramblers and, additionally, can be grown as shrubs.

The Multiflora ramblers, of robust character and sound good health, are frequently tolerant of the most unfavourable of conditions, and bloom profusely in early or mid-summer. However, they usually have stiffer growth than other rambler roses and require more extensive pruning to ensure the regular development of flowers.

'Aglaia' ('Yellow Rambler')

Schmitt, France, introduced by P. Lambert in 1896   2.5 × 1.8m (8 × 6ft)

Although no longer in cultivation, it was important historically for its role in Pemberton's crosses in the creation of his charming *moschata* hybrids in the 1920s, including the renowned 'Penelope', 'Felicia', and 'Cornelia'. It bore small, semi-double, primrose-yellow flowers in early summer. A rambler with few thorns, glossy and pale green leaves, coppery when young.

ORIGIN: *Rosa multiflora* × 'Rêve d'Or'

'Blush Rambler'

B. R. Cant, Great Britain, 1903   4 × 3m (12 × 10ft)

A strong and vigorous rambler which enjoyed popularity in the 1920s and was much grown in cottage gardens. Blooms are cupped, semi-double, blush-pink, deliciously fragrant, and in large cascading trusses. Stems almost thornless, with abundant light green leaves.

ORIGIN: 'Crimson Rambler' × 'The Garland'

'Goldfinch'

William Paul, Great Britain, 1907   5 × 3m (15 × 10ft)

A typical Multiflora, one of the best of the group, bearing clusters of golden buds which open in mid-summer, to small, very pretty, cupped, semi-double blooms of pale primrose-yellow fading to ivory. Very fragrant, with a rich fruity scent that carries well. Stems are almost thornless, leaves glossy. A less popular sport of 'Goldfinch', 'Ghislaine de Fligonde', deserves greater recognition. Introduced by Turbat in 1916, it is less vigorous, and can be grown as a large shrub; it is covered in early summer with large clusters of brilliant yellow blooms. Almost thornless, with broad glossy leaves.

'Goldfinch'

'Rambling Rector'

Prior to 1912   6 × 3m (20 × 10ft)

A rampant climber, with very thorny stems, most often seen,
and to good effect, rambling through robust, old trees. Produces
a profusion of small, semi-double, deliciously scented blooms,
in large trusses, cream, fading to white, with golden stamens at
the centre. Bears a crop of small, decorative hips in autumn.
Leaves are plentiful, small, hairy, grey-green.

'Russelliana' ('Old Spanish Rose', 'Russell's Cottage Rose', 'Souvenir de la Bataille de Marengo')

Discovered in Spain, 1837   6 × 3m (20 × 10ft)

Its many names bear witness to its immense popularity in the
past. The small, flat, very double, and strongly fragrant blooms
are carried in large clusters, and produced in great profusion in
mid-summer; crimson on emergence, they later fade with purplish tones. A tough, vigorous and hardy rose, with thorny
stems, and coarse dark leaves.
ORIGIN: It is thought to be a cross between *Rosa multiflora* and
Rosa setigera

'Seagull'

Pritchard 1907   5 × 4m (15 × 12ft)

Superb rambler with pure white, fragrant flowers with golden
stamens and borne in large trusses.

'Tea Rambler'

William Paul, Great Britain, 1904   3.5 × 2.5m (11 × 8ft)

A pleasing rose, with medium-sized, double, salmon-pink flowers, scented, early in bloom and slightly repeating.
ORIGIN: 'Crimson Rambler' × a Tea Rose

'The Garland'

Wells, Great Britain, 1835   6 × 3m (20 × 10ft)

A deservedly well-known rose, and a favourite of Gertrude
Jekyll. Long, pliable stems, well furnished with hooked thorns,
bear garlands of delightful, semi-double, blush-pink to cream
flowers, with a pervasive scent of orange blossoms, in early
summer. A good crop of tiny red hips follow in autumn.
ORIGIN: *Rosa moschata* × *Rosa multiflora*

'The Garland'

'Veilchenblau'

J. C. Schmidt, Germany, 1909

4 × 3.5m (12 × 11ft)

Optimistically called 'Blue Rose'; bears large clusters of very
small, semi-double blooms; violet-purple, flecked white at the
centre, and fading to lilac-grey. Has a very fresh scent of apples
which carries well when plants are in full bloom in early
summer. Stems are bright green, almost thornless, arching and
vigorous, the foliage ample and glossy. A very showy rambler,
at its best when associated with creamy flowered specimens.
Should be grown in part or dappled shade.

ORIGIN: 'Crimson Rambler' × 'Erinnerung an Brod'

'Veilchenblau'

ROSA SEMPER-VIRENS

Described by Dioscorides and Pliny, *Rosa sempervirens* is native around the Mediterranean basin. It has beautiful evergreen or semi-evergreen foliage, very graceful in leaf, with 5–7 long, lance-shaped, very glossy green leaflets. A scrambling or climbing species, it has smooth stems, or bears broad-based, hooked thorns, and in early and mid-summer carries panicles of single, slightly fragrant white flowers, followed in autumn by small, rounded orange-red hips. Although its hybrid progeny are relatively few, they have made an important contribution to gardens. One of the few which remain is the glorious 'Félicité et Perpétue'. This was a member of a small group created by A. A. Jacques – head gardener to Louis-Philippe, Duke of Orléans and future King of France – between 1820 and 1830. 'Flora', 'Princess Louise', and 'Princess Mary' may still be found on the market with diligent searching, but they are virtually unknown. But two of these varieties have not been forgotten. In 1954, the rosarian Roy E. Shepherd suggested that, although this species was first described in 1623 (as *R. moschata sempervirens*) and reached England before 1629, its use in hybridising was confined to a comparative few years and its hybrids were mostly originated by rose nurseries in France.

'Adélaide d'Orléans'

A. A. Jacques, France, 1826   5 × 3m (15 × 10ft) or more

A beautiful and refined rambler, with lush foliage, evergreen in mild climates. Bears cascading clusters of dainty, rose-tinted buds, which open to well-shaped, semi-double blooms of soft powder-pink, fading to white, and with an unmistakable fragrance of primroses. Blooms only at mid-summer, and is susceptible to mildew. May be cut to the ground in severe frosts. Its long trailing shoots are also attractive and reveal reddish prickles and small, dark green leaves. It is ideal for clothing arches and pergolas.

'Félicité et Perpétue'

A. A. Jacques, France, 1828   5 × 3m (15 × 10ft) or more

Dedicated to Jacques's daughters, this adorable rose has been in cultivation for over one hundred and fifty years and despite its borderline hardiness, is unlikely to be forgotten. It bears its seductive blooms in clusters at the ends of slender, arching stems, pink in bud, opening to small, full-petalled rosettes, creamy with a pink-flushed reverse, and with the delicate texture of tissue, and a delicate scent of primrose. Stems thornless, leaves small, dark, glossy, semi-evergreen. Ideal specimen for growing through trees. Its sport 'Little White Pet' is similar, but smaller and recurrent, and very useful as a ground cover.
ORIGIN: *Rosa sempervirens × Rosa chinensis*

'Adélaide d'Orléans'

ROSA
WICHURAIANA

Rosa *wichuraiana*, native to China, Korea, Taiwan and Japan, was discovered in Asia by the German botanist Max Ernst Wichur and arrived in Europe in 1886. It is one of the most vigorous species; in its natural habitat it is observed growing along the ground, creeping up and over whatever crosses its path with flexible, smooth, green shoots, using hooked thorns to climb when it can. Like *R. sempervirens* it retains its leaves, which are bright, shining green, for all or most of the year. The single, scented blooms are approximately 5cm (2in) across, white with long golden stamens at the centre, carried from mid- to late summer, and followed by dark, ovoid hips. It may reach 6m (20ft) or more, given support. The species is rarely grown, but many of its hybrids are, including some of the most beautiful and tenacious of ramblers. One name in particular is linked to them, that of Monsieur Barbier who began work at the beginning of this century; he is unlikely to be forgotten, if for no other reason than that 'Albéric Barbier' and – introduced later – 'Albertine' were named after him, although these are thought to be descendants of the very similar *Rosa luciae*. Several splendid hybrids have also been created in the United States, thanks mainly to the dedicated and detailed work of Walsh, Manda and Van Fleet.

The Wichuriana ramblers have a great deal to offer in modern gardens; these are plants which are renowned for their robust good health, their glossy foliage, and the explosion of bloom during summer. They are vigorous and cold

hardy, and are extremely useful for clothing trellis, pillar and pergola, or for covering slopes and banks. They are unbeatable for covering unsightly fences or buildings, providing a rapid transformation of the unspeakably ugly to the breathtakingly beautiful.

They are best left unpruned, other than to remove dead or over exuberant growth.

'Albéric Barbier'

Barbier, France, 1900   5 × 3m (15 × 10ft) or more

A world-famous favourite, a very reliable large-flowered rambler, of broadly spreading habit with rather stiff stems and healthy, glossy, dark green foliage. It bears double blooms, neatly quartered at first, later rather muddled, opening creamy white, flushed yellow in the petal folds, and with a pleasant green-apple scent. Blooms for about 34 weeks from early summer. It is ideal for covering unsightly buildings and large fences, as well as climbing into trees. It has also been allowed to sprawl over the ground to create a feast of shoots and colour. However, the shoots do not totally cover the ground, and hand-weeding is essential to keep the area tidy. It is therefore not wholly successful as a ground-cover plant.

ORIGIN: *Rosa wichuraiana* or *R. luciae* × 'Shirley Hibberd'

'Albéric Barbier'

'Albertine'

Barbier, France, 1921   5 × 3m (15 × 10ft) or more

A very popular rambler valued for the clusters of voluptuous, double blooms, of almost Tea rose shape, in warm peach-pink, particularly well-scented in the evening, with a sweet, fruity fragrance. A short flowering season, like 'Albéric Barbier' and rather susceptible to mildew after blooming. The stems are strong but pliant, well furnished with hooked thorns, the glossy leaves are coppery when young, bright green when mature. Well-branched and bushy, strong enough to be grown as a free-standing, and broadly spreading shrub.

ORIGIN: *Rosa wichuraiana* or *R. luciae* × 'Mrs Arthur Robert Waddell'

'American Pillar'

W. Van Fleet, USA, 1902, introduced in 1908   5 × 3m (15 × 10ft) or more

A small-flowered rambler, once very popular, but considered somewhat vulgar by connoisseurs; Vita Sackville-West described it as 'horrid'. In truth, it is once-blooming, lacks scent, and is prone to mildew, and has probably been superseded by other, better reds which are reliably recurrent. Nevertheless, it bears a showy profusion of small, single, rosy-red blooms with a white eye, and has robust and vigorous stems well suited to pillars and pergolas. It has the bonus of bearing red hips in autumn.

ORIGIN: (*Rosa wichuraiana* × *Rosa setigera*) × 'Red Letter Day'

'Auguste Gervais'

Barbier, France, 1918   5 × 2.5m (15 × 8ft) or more

Rather large, delicate, semi-double blooms of coppery pink with salmon shadings, fading to creamy white, and with very dark orange-gold stamens at the centre; good fragrance, and attractive glossy foliage on robust stems. Blooms once, but over a long period in summer.

ORIGIN: *Rosa wichuraiana* × 'Le Progrès'

'Débutante'

Walsh, USA, 1902   4 × 3m (15 × 10ft)

An excellent, healthy and vigorous rambler, producing masses of small, double, pink blooms against glossy, dark green leaves. A slight fragrance reminiscent of *Rosa rubiginosa*. Once flowering but with a few blooms later in the season.

ORIGIN: *Rosa wichuraiana* × 'Baroness Rothschild'

'Dorothy Perkins'

Jackson & Perkins, USA, 1901   5 × 3m (15 × 10ft)

Enormously popular in the past, but less so today, probably because of its susceptibility to mildew and lack of scent. Carries large sprays of small, double, pink blooms with a blue undertone, in great profusion in early summer. Pliable and arching stems, with glossy, dark green leaves. It is a popular variety but does need good soil conditions to ensure longevity and regular development of flowers. The beautiful, pale pink 'Lady Godiva' is a sport of 'Dorothy Perkins'.

ORIGIN: *Rosa wichuraiana* × 'Mme Gabriel Luizet'

'Evangeline'

Walsh, USA, 1906   5 × 3m (15 × 10ft)

A rambling rose with healthy, leathery leaves and clusters of small, single, sweetly scented, pale pink blooms, veined darker pink. Blooms once, quite late in the season; the single blooms are unusual in a *wichuraiana* hybrid.

ORIGIN: *Rosa wichuraiana* × 'Crimson Rambler'

'Dorothy Perkins'

'Excelsa' ('Red Dorothy Perkins') 　🚫 🖼 ✿ ❖

Walsh, USA, 1909 　　　　　　　　5 × 3m (15 × 10ft)

Resembles a crimson-flowered 'Dorothy Perkins', bearing
numerous, many-petalled pompons, with white highlights at
the centre. Very floriferous but not repeating. A strong rambler,
with flexible stems and glossy leaves.

'François Juranville' 　　　　　　　🌸 🖼 ✿ ❖

Barbier, France, 1906 　　　　　　　6 × 3m (20 × 10ft)

A distinctive rambler which deserves a place in any garden, to
scramble over a fence, tree, or pergola. Exceptionally beautiful
blooms, with a fruity fragrance, medium-sized and double, rich
salmon-pink shaded with darker tones, opening flat with slightly quilled petals. The main flush of flowers is carried in early
summer, a few are occasionally produced later. With long, arching stems, purple brown, with few prickles and plentiful leaves,
bronze tinted when young. Do not plant it against a wall or
fence as a good circulation of air is needed to prevent the onset
of mildew, an unsightly disease.

ORIGIN: *Rosa wichuraiana* × 'Mme Laurette Messimy'

'Gardenia' 　　　　　　　　　　　🚫 🖼

W. A. Manda, USA, 1899 　　　　　　6 × 4m (20 × 12ft)

Not much seen in cultivation; a graceful, long-flowering rose,
with dainty, pointed, yellow buds, and shapely, very full and
quartered blooms, creamy white with a green-apple scent.
Vigorous and pliant stems, and very attractive small, glossy,
dark green leaves.

ORIGIN: *Rosa wichuraiana* × 'Perle des Jardins'

149

'Gerbe Rose'
Fauque, France, 1904   3.5 × 2.5m (11 × 8ft)

Not really true to the type, being of a less strong growth and with stiff stems, it is a pleasing rose for the lovely, flat, double blooms, nicely quartered, clear pink fading to cream at the base, and with a peony-like fragrance. Not profusely blooming, but graceful, delicate, and recurrent throughout summer.
ORIGIN: *Rosa wichuraiana* × 'Baroness Rothschild'

'Jersey Beauty'
W. A. Manda, USA, 1899   5 × 3m (15 × 10ft)

A vigorous rambler, with plentiful glossy, dark green leaves, and bearing large sprays of single, fragrant, creamy blooms.
ORIGIN: *Rosa wichuraiana* × 'Perle des Jardins'

'Léontine Gervais'
Barbier, France, 1903   6 × 3m (20 × 10ft)

An appealing rose with large, fragrant, double blooms, slightly and pleasantly muddled when fully open, and of lovely colouring: coppery orange in bud opening to warm apricot-pink, with deeper shading in the petal folds. A very well branched plant with flexible stems and beautiful, glossy, dark green leaves.
ORIGIN: *Rosa wichuraiana* × 'Souvenir de Cathérine Guillot'

'May Queen'

'May Queen'
W. A. Manda, USA., 1898   5 × 2.5m (15 × 8ft)

An attractive rambler which deserves the favour it enjoys. Will scramble freely over slopes, or make a dense, free-standing and sprawling shrub in the wild garden. Bears small clusters of cupped, quartered blooms of great beauty and with a fruity scent: clear lilac-pink tinted mauve with age. The generous first blooming is sometimes followed by a few later flowers. Robust, vigorous, free-flowering, and very hardy.
ORIGIN: *Rosa wichuraiana* × 'Champion of the World'

'Minnehaha'

Walsh, USA, 1905
5 × 2.5m (15 × 8ft)

Popular in the past and difficult to imagine why it is no longer
widely grown. It bears splendid, cascading clusters of small,
double blooms, packed with deep rose-pink petals, which in
favourable conditions are carried over long periods in summer.
There is only a light scent. Leaves are plentiful, small, glossy,
and dark green.

ORIGIN: *Rosa wichuraiana*

'Paul Transon'

Barbier, France, 1900
5 × 2.5m (15 × 8ft)

Buds of deep orange-pink open to medium-sized, flat and double blooms, soft salmon-pink flushed copper, with a pleasing
apple fragrance. The main flush of bloom is in early summer,
but with regular production of fewer flowers later in the season.
A strong, bushy rambler, with glossy leaves tinted bronze,
requiring a sheltered position and protection from mildew.

ORIGIN: *Rosa wichuraiana* × 'L'Idéal'

'Sander's White'

Sander & Sons, Great Britain, 1912
3.5 × 2.5m (11 × 8ft)

An excellent rambler, one of the best whites. Large cascading
trusses of pure white rosettes, intensely fragrant, in fine contrast
with glossy, bright green foliage. It is grown to great effect as a
standard at the Roseraie de l'Hay, near Paris. Makes good
ground cover. Stems well-furnished with strong thorns.

'Sander's White'

ROSA
ARVENSIS

Rosa arvensis is extremely widespread in Europe, from Iceland to Spain in the west, and from Germany to Greece in the east, and it is commonly found in southern Britain. The Field Rose is frequently encountered in hedgerows, with long, trailing, arching stems bearing beautiful single, scented pure white flowers in early to mid-summer, followed by small, globose, red hips. Its primary contribution to gardens has been as the small group of roses of Scottish origin – though curiously born of seeds sent from Canada – known as Ayrshire Roses; the eponymous 'Ayrshire Rose', a double form of the species, was grown from the end of the 18th century. Other varieties came later, but there are very few left in our gardens. Gertrude Jekyll praises two in particular: 'Dundee Rambler' and 'Bennett's Seedling'. They are roses which should be left to grow in the most natural way possible, climbing over hedges or shrubs as their fancy takes them.

'Bennett's Seedling'

Bennett, Great Britain, 1840

6 × 3m (20 × 10ft)

Of unknown origin, probably a spontaneous, double form of *Rosa arvensis*, bearing large clusters of very pretty, many-petalled, white blooms. Very fragrant and very hardy.

'Dundee Rambler'

Martin, Scotland, 1850 but known prior to 1838

6 × 3m (20 × 10ft)

Small, very double, white flowers flushed with pink at the petal margins, in large sprays.

ORIGIN: probably a cross between *Rosa arvensis* and a Noisette

'Ruga'

Prior to 1830

3 × 5m (10 × 15ft) or more

A very strong rambler, raised in Italy, with large, loose trusses of open-cupped, semi-double, sweetly scented blooms, clear pink fading to cream.

ORIGIN: *Rosa arvensis* × a China Rose

'Splendens' ('Ayrshire Splendens', 'Myrrh-scented Rose')

Prior to 1838

6 × 3m (20 × 10ft)

Very strongly scented of myrrh, and very pretty. Buds are crimson-tinted, opening to cup-shaped, semi-double blooms, white, blush-pink at the petal edge and on the reverse, packed with golden stamens at the centre. Stems and leaves are dark green. A very good ground cover rose.

'Ruga'

ROSA SOULIEANA

'Kew Rambler'

Native to Tibet and western China, where it was discovered by Abbi Souli, and introduced into Europe in 1896; it made its way to Kew in 1899. A very dense but dainty shrub, with slender, arching stems, large yellowish thorns, and soft, glaucous leaves divided into nine oval leaflets. It bears clusters of numerous single blooms, yellow in bud, and fading to white on opening, followed by small, oval, orange-red hips. It blooms freely in mid-summer. Not very hardy although its varieties are more so.

'Kew Rambler'
Introduced in 1913   6 × 3.5m (20 × 11ft)

In cultivation at the Royal Botanic Gardens, Kew, in 1912, the best rambler derived from *Rosa soulieana*. It has a very graceful habit, elegant foliage, and delightful clusters of small, scented, single flowers, pink with a white eye. Thorny and rather stiff stems; fruits well in autumn, bearing orange-red hips. Once-flowering in early summer. As its name indicates, it was raised at the Royal Botanic Gardens, Kew.
ORIGIN: *Rosa soulieana* × 'Hiawatha'

'Ohio'

Shepherd, USA, 1949

2 × 0.9m (6 × 3ft)

A modern rambler, included here by virtue of its parentage. A tall shrub, with long, arching shoots produced from the base, clothed in semi-double, bright red blooms, repeating from early summer. A very hardy, free-flowering plant, useful where space is confined, and suitable for pot cultivation.

ORIGIN: *Rosa soulieana* × a 'Grüss an Teplitz' seedling

'Wickwar'

Steadman, Great Britain, 1960

2.5 × 2m (8 × 6ft)

Another modern, and very beautiful rose, making a dense, bushy shrub or rambler, with copious grey-green leaves, and very fragrant, creamy flowers with an attractive and very prominent boss of stamens.

ORIGIN: *Rosa brunonii* × *Rosa soulieana*

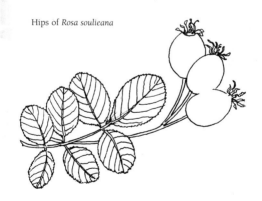

Hips of *Rosa soulieana*

Care and cultivation

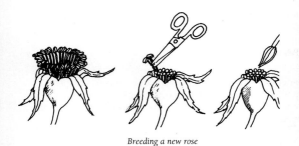

Breeding a new rose

Removing a side bud to obtain larger blooms

Dead heading

Sucker to be removed

Correct cut in pruning

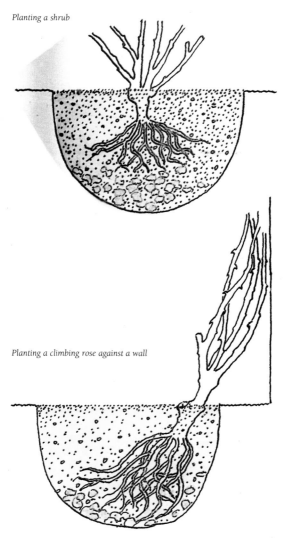

Planting a shrub

Planting a climbing rose against a wall

Bibliography

Graham Stuart Thomas
The Old Shrub Roses, Phoenix House, London, 1955
Climbing Roses Old and New, Phoenix House, London, 1965

Gertrude Jekyll, E. Mawley
Roses for English Gardens, Country Life, 1902

Ellen A. Willmott
The Genus Rose, London, 1914

Peter Beales
Classic Roses, Collins Harvill, London, 1985

David Austin
The Heritage of the Rose, Antique Collectors' Club, 1987

Michael Gibson
The Book of Classic Old Roses, Idea Books

Trevor Griffiths
My World of Old Roses, Whitcoules, 1983
The Book of Old Roses, Michael Joseph, London, 1984

Nancy Steen
The Charm of Old Roses, Herbert Jenkins, London, 1967

Allen Paterson
The History of the Rose, Collins, London, 1983

S. Sitwell, J. Russell
Old Garden Roses, George Rainbird, 1955

R. Philips, M. Rix
Roses, Pan Books Ltd.

S.M. Gault, P.M. Synge
The Dictionary of Roses in Colour, Michael Joseph,
London, 1984

E.A. Bunyard
Old Garden Roses, Collingridge

G. Edwards
Wild and Old Garden Roses, David & Charles,
Newton Abbot

Acknowledgements

Photography:

Rose Barni, Pistoia pages 10–11, 18, 37, 38, 41, 48, 49, 51 (Salet), 55, 63, 67, 70 (La Reine Victoria), 72, 75, 78, 85, 87, 90, 92 (Frau Karl Druschki), 95 (Paul Neyron), 117 (Lady Penzance), 125 (Conrad Ferdinand Meyer), 127, 134 (Anemone Rose), 149; **Rolph Blakstad** pages 2, 4, 16, 27, 28 (Gloire de Guilan), 30, 31, 32, 42, 56, 57, 77, 84, 91, 96, 114, 132; **Alberto Mondellini** pages 21, 22, 23, 36, 59 (Mutabilis), 69, 82, 93, 95 (Reine des Violettes), 97, 98, 101, 102, 105, 107 (Gertrude Jekyll), 108, 112–113, 117 (Lord Penzance), 121, 128, 133, 134 (Ramona), 145, 146, 150, 151, 153; **Mario Sabbieti** pages 17, 19, 28 (Celsiana), 29, 43, 47, 51 (Zoe), 59 (Old Blush), 64, 70 (Louise Odier), 71, 73, 99, 103, 104, 106, 107 (Heritage), 110, 111, 115, 141, 143, 147, 151, 154, 165; **Vera Sandri Rigo** pages 20, 109, 125 (Blank Double de Coubert), 138–139; **Marco Volpati** pages 92 (Ferdinand Pichard), 126; **Archivio Garzanti** pages 35, 60, 120, 136, 137, 159

Colour drawings by **Pierre-Joseph Redouté**

Black and white illustrations by **Orietta Sala**

Parson's Pink China

Index

Suppliers of old-fashioned roses

David Austin Roses, Bowling Green Lane, Albrighton, Wolverhampton, WV7 3HB

Peter Beales, Old London Road, Attleborough, Norfolk, NR17 1AY

Gandy's Roses Ltd, North Kilworth (Lutterworth), Leics LE17 6HZ

Apuldram Roses, Chichester, Apuldram Lane, Dell Quay, West Sussex, PO20 7EF

Stydd Nursery, Dept R, Ribchester, Nr Preston, Lancs PR3 3YN

Old Garden Roses, Acton Beauchamps, Worchester (TR) WR6 5AE

Cranborne Manor Garden Centre, Cranborne, Dorset

Cocker Jamas and Son, Whitemyres, Lang Stracht, Aberdeen, AB9 2XH, Scotland

Cant's of Colchester, Dept R, Nayland Road, Mile End, Colchester, CO4 5EB

Bowood Garden Centre, Calne, Wiltshire

Trevor White Old Fashioned Roses, Chelt Hurst, Sewell Road, Norwich NR3 4BP

Bloomingdales Garden Centre, 150 Staines Road, Laleham, Middlesex

Mermaid